Vintage
Paris Couture

THE FRENCH WOMAN'S GUIDE TO SHOPPING

Jessica Clayton

Vintage Paris Couture

THE FRENCH WOMAN'S GUIDE TO SHOPPING

Universe

Contents

Preface

My own enthusiasm for the wardrobes of the past was awakened on childhood Sunday afternoons, when I avidly watched matinee screenings of black-and-white Hollywood films from the '30s and '40s. My fascination was not so much with the film stars as with their clothes, which I found wonderful. They made me dream. This in turn made me beg tirelessly for visits to the attics and basements of elderly relatives. When I got what I wanted, it was like Christmas and I would ecstatically sashay around all day in Grandma's outsized ball gown. Gone was the nine-year-old girl—the dress had transformed me into a sophisticated princess. When, as a teenager, I found my way to the shops whose wares were then known as secondhand, I filled my wardrobe with a motley collection of clothes from yesteryear. A very special delight overcame me when a 1930s silk evening gown, cleverly cut on the bias, proved a perfect fit. The thought that the dress had once draped another body, similar to mine, sent my imagination wild. What adventures might the dress have had? What floors had it swept along? Whose heads had it turned in the street? It was as if the fabric had a memory of its own.

Similar flights of fancy may go some way toward explaining the special value attached to clothes that were once owned or worn by a famous person. It's not just the finery you're buying, but a part of the life it belonged to as well. In some mysterious way, the garment gives its new owner access to a world that would otherwise be closed to her. There are similarities here with medieval relic cults—the belief that an apparently inanimate object is made animate by its owner.

Other eras and styles have a further universe of fantasy to offer. The design of the clothes defines our roles as men and women. The woman who pulls the belt tight around her waist in a '50s gown is not the same kind of woman as the one who dons a '70s YSL tuxedo. The man who is crazy about '70s biker jackets is not the same as the one who seeks out English tweed classics, or smoking jackets of velvet or satin. Vintage gives you the opportunity to play with these roles. Using vintage clothes, you can define who you are, or your mood for the day. Just imagine, you can begin your day in a slender '20s outfit, only to transform yourself into a '50s rocker girl after lunch, or into a '60s flower child. In the evening you can bring out the woman in yourself with an elegant '30s dress.

But vintage is more than that. It is a reaction against the ubiquitous uniform of Western culture—a result of the virtually dictatorial influence of large multinational clothing chains on what we wear. Vintage gives us the real thing instead of copies of varying quality. But above all, it gives us the possibility of being unique. It is also a reaction against consumer society with its culture of "buy, use once, and discard." By exploring and emptying forgotten wardrobes in attics and basements, traders in vintage clothes are salvaging a part of our cultural heritage and preserving a craftsmanship tradition for posterity. Without Fortuny's "Delphos" dress in pleated silk, Issey Miyake's "Pleats Please" might never have been.

Finally, vintage may be seen as a way of searching for one's roots (or others' roots)—a natural consequence of a society in which everything moves faster and faster, and whose future appears increasingly unclear.

Secondhand, retro, retro deluxe, charity-shop clothes, *fripes*, vintage. There's no shortage of names for it, and which one of them does greatest justice to the vintage phenomenon is a matter of some debate. Perhaps "retro" is the name that best describes something "qui marque un retour en arrière, reprend ou imite un style passé" (as defined in *Petit Robert*: "which marks a flashback, which appropriates or copies a past style"). In recent years, the term "vintage" has become increasingly common despite the fact that many people feel it does not belong in the clothes context. The word itself is of English origin, and most commonly used about wine from a given year. According to the *Dictionary Thesaurus*, the adjective "vintage" denotes "something of high quality esp. something from the past."

The most suitable definition of the term in the current context comes from the *Dictionnaire international de la mode*: "Le terme vintage a fini par désigner tout un jeu d'apparences utilisant des vêtements anciens, du mélange de fripes et de vêtements neuf portés au quotidien jusqu'aux pièces exceptionnelles" ("the term vintage has come to designate a whole range of looks that make use of old clothes, from everyday mixing of flea-market finds with new clothes to wearing rare haute couture garments").

How the term is used and understood by people in the fashion business, or in the street, is a different matter entirely. Here in France, for instance, I have heard the word associated with the number twenty (*vingt*)—the idea being that the clothes thus termed should be at least twenty years old.

So what is meant by "vintage"? One way of describing the phenomenon is "clothes that have been given a second life." This is an incomplete description, however, as many garments are given a second life without being classifiable as vintage. To merit that label, the clothes need to be of a certain age, i.e., come from a decade other than the current one. They should furthermore possess some measure of quality, and perhaps it is this aspect that most complicates things. Quality is, of course, a characteristic open to different definitions and perceptions. For instance, there are traders who focus on mass-produced clothes from the '60s, '70s, and '80s, and who argue that it is this style in itself that represents quality. This idea is rejected by others, who choose a narrower definition of what should be regarded as quality. Craftsmanship and material are decisive factors for them, along with the garment's design in its historical context. Yet others associate the term with designer clothes from the twentieth century. The common denominator of all these interpretations is that vintage concerns a rediscovery and a reappraisal of a style that has been forgotten or declared dreadful. If someone had told me during the glamorous '80s that the loud style of that particular era would, in a couple of decades' time, come to fill the shelves of vintage shops and make young vintage consumers fall over themselves in admiration, I would most likely not have believed them.

The phenomenon of vintage—retro, secondhand, or whatever you choose to call it—emerged in the heyday of the 1970s hippie movement, when granny's lace dresses from the previous turn of the century suddenly became hard currency. Films such as *The Great Gatsby* and *Bonnie and Clyde* made people covet '20s outfits, and had women wearing berets as never before. For a long time, though, buyers were a mostly modest group of faithful enthusiasts, people from the theatre, the film industry, and museums. It wasn't until Julia Roberts strode onto the red carpet on Oscars night in 2001 wearing a 1992 creation by Valentino that it became *comme il faut* to wear vintage clothes on public occasions!

It is my fascination with older clothes, and all the dreams they can evoke, that I want to share. One way to do so has been to write this guide to all the vintage hideaways that Paris holds. In it, I have brought together antique clothes from the eighteenth and nineteenth centuries with masterpieces of haute couture, creations of anonymous seamstresses, and mass-produced clothes from the various decades of the twentieth century—from the most exclusive shops the world of vintage has to offer to the cheapest flea market stalls.

Jessica Clayton

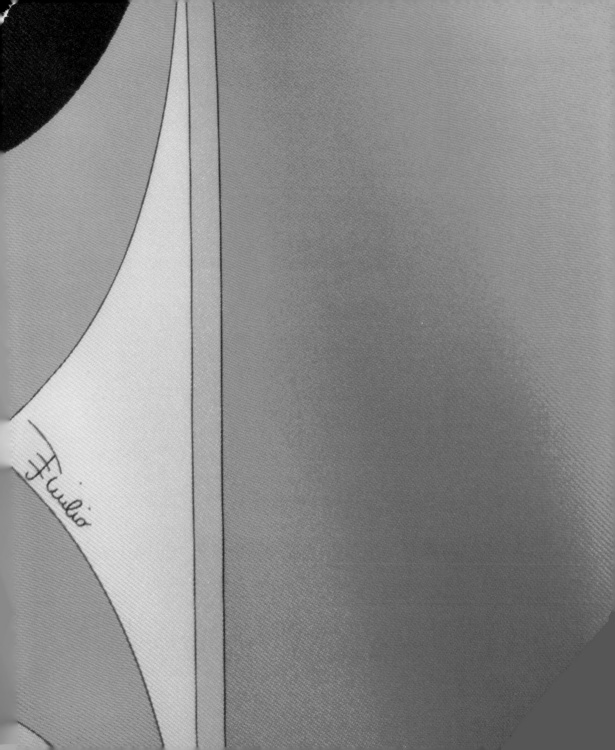

1st & 2nd
arrondissements

Neila Vintage & Design

Between the Tuileries Gardens and the many shops of rue du Faubourg Saint-Honoré is rue du Mont Thabor, where Neila Jaziri opened her vintage and design shop in April 2007. She has a background as an actress and interior designer, and was inspired to open her shop during a visit to New York. Neila specializes in vintage couture and haute couture from 1900 until the glamorous 1980s. On her hangers you will find designs by masters such as Yves Saint Laurent, Chanel, Balenciaga, Elsa Schiaparelli, Dior, Hermès, and Nina Ricci. Dresses sell for between €500 and €3,000, but for a haute couture design by Balenciaga the price will be in the €5,000–7,000 range. Items of haute couture jewelry are about €900–1,000, and *bijoux fantaisie* about €200. Neila herself has a weakness for the 1980s, for 1960s haute couture, and for American glamour jewelry.

28, rue du Mont Thabor, 75001 Paris
Monday–Saturday 10:30 A.M.–1 P.M. / 2 P.M.–7:30 P.M.
T +33 1 42 96 88 70 / jaziri_neila@yahoo.fr
M° Tuileries

Break

Musée de la Mode et du Textile
The museum opened in 1986 and owns one of the biggest collections of costumes and textiles in the world. The historical costumes date from the Regency period to the present day. The museum also possesses collections of the work of great designers such as Paul Poiret, Madeleine Vionnet, Elsa Schiaparelli, and Christian Dior.
Palais du Louvre
107, rue de Rivoli, 75001 Paris
Tuesday–Friday 11:30 A.M.–6 P.M.
Saturday–Sunday 10 A.M.–6 P.M.
T +33 1 44 55 57 50
www.lesartsdecoratifs.fr
M° Palais Royal Musée du Louvre

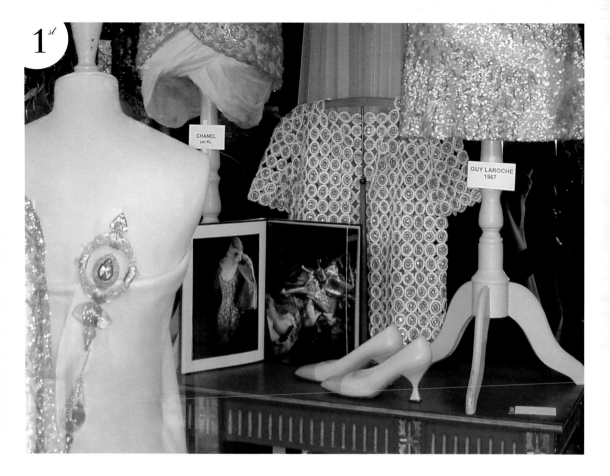

Within the image: CHANEL par KL · GUY LAROCHE 1967

Didier Ludot

Didier Ludot is the uncrowned king of vintage. After more than thirty years in the business, he has ensconced himself at the very top. In his area, he is unique in the world. He deals primarily in French vintage couture from the 1920s until the present. He has three shops under the arcades of the Palais Royal: one for accessories and vintage couture, one for haute couture, and one that has the same name and contents as his book, *La Petite Robe Noire*.

The shops have the same very exclusive character and customers include collectors, designers hungry for inspiration, and posh folk from all over the world. They all enjoy browsing Didier's treasures. And they are spoiled for choice, with the most fabulous creations for women by masters such as Courrèges, Chanel, Lanvin, Balenciaga, Madame Grès, Marcel Rochas, Dior, and Poiret. It is clear that only the very best is good enough for Monsieur Ludot.

Jardins du Palais Royal,
20 and 24, Galerie Montpensier, 75001 Paris
Monday–Saturday 10:30 A.M.–7 P.M.
T +33 1 42 96 06 56 / www.didierludot.com
M° Palais Royal Musée du Louvre

La Petite Robe Noire

The third shop of Didier Ludot, **La Petite Robe Noire**, lies just across the gardens of the Palais Royal. It is a shop filled with little black dresses. However, in this shop he sells not only vintage dresses but also his own collection. Monsieur Ludot's source of inspiration is, of course, dresses from previous eras.

Jardins du Palais Royal,
125, Galerie Valois, 75001 Paris
Monday–Saturday 11 A.M.–7 P.M.
T +33 1 40 15 01 04
M° Palais Royal Musée du Louvre

Iglaïne

Dominique Cesselin—known among her suppliers as *l'emmerdeuse* (the pain in the . . .) because she refuses to buy by the weight and instead hand-picks each garment—has run her shop for sixteen years. It is not a large space, but it still holds almost ten thousand garments. Most of these are found at the back of the shop. They are cleverly hung on a mechanized clothes carousel salvaged from a defunct dry cleaner. Just press a button and the carousel starts up, and when something that interests you passes, hit the stop button. Dominique believes that all eras have their specific charm—the range of her selection extends from the beginning of the twentieth century to the 1980s. New items are added every week. Her shop is frequented by tourists, stylists, designers, stage and film costume designers, and others passionate about vintage clothes. Prices range from €20 to €900 for Courrèges dresses in mint condition. Dominique is particularly proud of a Pucci handbag.

12, rue de la Grande Truanderie, 75001 Paris
Monday—Saturday 11 A.M.—7 P.M.
T +33 1 42 36 19 91 / iglaine@wanadoo.fr
M° Les Halles or Etienne Marcel

Gabrielle Geppert

Globetrotter Gabrielle Geppert opened her first shop just over four years ago. It is a small shop with lots of light and a colorful and feminine selection of women's clothes and accessories.

The small space is literally brimming, with collections of bags and shoes filling the walls. Gabrielle's interest in vintage clothes began early—she took to wearing them in her teens. She has a soft spot for items from the turn of the last century such as the black pearl-covered capes known as *visites*. But she is also fond of the 1980s crop of designers including Mugler and Alaïa. She does not seek out labels, but rather buys things she likes. However, these often turn out to be from well-known labels, as is apparent from her display.

She spends much of her time buying, so the selection in the shop is constantly being renewed. It extends from the turn of the last century until the present; prices range from €10 to €4,000.

At the end of 2006 Gabrielle expanded her business by opening a second shop a few doors down the arcade, where she specializes in exclusive, carefully chosen garments and accessories. This shop is particularly recommended for connoisseurs looking for that extra something.

At the Printemps exhibition in autumn 2005, Gabrielle demonstrated her gift for finding and creating individual, vibrant vintage collections by showing a collection of 1970s clothes and accessories with a folkloristic touch.

Jardins du Palais Royal,
31 and 34, Galerie Montpensier, 75001 Paris
Monday–Saturday 10 A.M.–7:30 P.M. and some Sundays
T +33 1 42 61 53 52 or +33 6 22 92 53 25
www.gabriellegeppert.com
M° Palais Royal Musée du Louvre

GABRIELLE
GEPPERT

Création & Diffusion Rag

Opened six years ago, **Création & Diffusion Rag** may be a small shop, but its contents have been chosen with care. About 70 percent of the garments are women's clothes, and the rest is menswear. Specialities include designer clothes and accessories from Dior, Leonard, Pucci, Yves Saint Laurent, and Courrèges. There are also marvelous kimonos imported directly from Japan. The clothes span the period from 1920 to 1980, and prices range from €30 to €1,200. One favorite is a black evening gown with sequins, a Courrèges design from the 1980s—Lady Di had an identical dress! Another is an exquisite little vanity bag by Paco Rabanne, for €450. The clientele is international and of all ages. There is a second **Rag** shop at 83, rue Saint-Martin (see pages 74–75), with a slightly different selection.

81, rue Saint-Honoré, 75001 Paris
Monday–Saturday 11 A.M.–7:30 P.M. / Sunday noon–7:30 P.M.
T +33 1 40 28 48 44
M° Les Halles

Son & Image

Son & Image has been in existence for fourteen years, and just opened a new shop in the third arrondissement. In France, this kind of secondhand shop is known as a *fripe*. It specializes in clothes from the 1950s, 1960s, and 1970s, and is unisex though menswear dominates. The selection combines jeans, leather, and army jackets with patterned shirts and flowery dresses. Garments are bought wholesale in Europe and America. Prices are low, and the clientele fairly young.

The second shop, across boulevard Sébastopol, opened in 2006. This shop is smaller, the period covered is somewhat narrower—clothes are mainly from the 1960s and 1970s—and the selection somewhat sharper. There are also more dresses and bags here than in the other shop. The aim has been to pick out the choice items and give them their own shop. But this is still a fripe, with reasonable prices.

※

85–87, rue Saint-Denis, 75001 Paris
Monday–Saturday 10:30 A.M.– 8 P.M. / Sunday 2 P.M.–8 P.M.
T +33 1 40 41 90 61
M° Les Halles

71, rue Quincampoix, 75003 Paris
Monday–Saturday noon–8 P.M.
T +33 1 42 79 16 89
M° Rambuteau

Fr / Jp Design & Vintage

Japanese owner Nobuko opened her 160 square feet to the world in January 2004. Her concept for the store is to mix vintage clothes from Europe with new designers from Japan. When she searches through the wardrobe of the twentieth century, she looks for clothes that match current trends. Nobuko's vintage collection is a small but quirky and varied selection of lace blouses from the turn of the century mixed with 1940s flower-pattern dresses, designer clothes from the 1960s, 1970s, and 1980s, plus a fair amount of bags, shoes, and boots. Prices start at €15 and end at €1,000. A silk blouse with lace from the early twentieth century costs €120; a skirt and blouse from Yves Saint Laurent €300. A 1970s trench coat by Celine sells for €300 as well. Shoes are between €30 and €150.

❧

8, rue La Vrillière (behind place des Victoires), 75001 Paris
Tuesday–Friday 11 A.M.–7:30 P.M. / Saturday 2 P.M.–7 P.M.
or by appointment
T +33 1 42 96 11 48
www.frjp-boutique.com / fr.jp@wanadoo.fr
M° Bourse

Oldies

Fred Touati has been in the textile business since the 1970s. Since then he and his family have also had their premises here in the heart of Sentier. In early 2007 he expanded the business by turning a part of the space into a secondhand shop selling clothes and accessories from the 1970s and 1980s. The main motives behind the project were to recycle clothes from the past and to return to the Sentier neighborhood's glorious past as a center of fashion in Paris. Prices are reasonable: €10 for a hat, €15 for silk shawls, and €35 to €75 for dresses. The most expensive items are leather jackets, at around €135. Women's clothes dominate, but there are men's clothes, too.

25, rue de Cléry, 75002 Paris
Monday–Friday 9:30 A.M.–1 P.M. / 2 P.M.–6 P.M.
Saturday 2 P.M.–7 P.M.
T +33 1 42 33 21 28
www.myspace.com/oldiesvintageclothes
M° Sentier

Break

La Bocca
Good Italian food on two floors.
59, rue Montmartre, 75002 Paris
Every day noon–2:30 P.M. / 8 P.M.–11:30 P.M.
Friday–Saturday until midnight
T +33 1 42 36 71 88
M° Sentier

Vintage 39-41 & 51-53

Yorham Douiev always dreamed about working with clothes. When his uncle introduced him to one of France's biggest wholesalers in the business, he knew it was vintage clothes to which he wanted to devote himself. He opened his shop at the end of February 2007, which makes it the youngest shop in this guide. Yorham has filled his 430 square feet with 1,500 garments, shawls, shoes, and bags from the 1960s, 1970s, 1980s, and 1990s. His selection is sourced mainly from America and Europe. Turnover is considerable, and new items are added all the time. The price range is €19–99.

A few steps down the passage you will find his second shop, a space dedicated to men.

39–41, passage Choiseul (women)
51–53, passage Choiseul (men), 75002 Paris
Monday–Friday 11 A.M.–7 P.M. / Saturday noon–7 P.M.
T +33 1 42 96 64 79 / vintageshop3941@yahoo.fr
M° Quatre Septembre or Pyramides

Breaks

Ultramod
One of the best notions shops.
The shop has been here since the early nineteenth century, and its interior is full of buttons, ribbons, lace, tassels, fringes, and much more. And a lot of it is vintage!
3 and 4, rue de Choiseul, 75002 Paris
Monday–Friday 10 A.M.–6 P.M.
T +33 1 42 96 98 30
M° Quatre Septembre

Higuma
A Japanese canteen with reasonable prices and delicious gyoza. Food is served throughout the day, so if you avoid the lunch rush you can have the place almost to yourself.
32 bis, rue Sainte-Anne, 75001 Paris
Every day 11:30 A.M.–10 P.M.
T +33 1 47 03 38 59
M° Pyramides or Quatre Septembre

Kiliwatch

Bernard Graf began his career in the Paris flea markets. Over the years, he acquired a number of stocks of old clothes. He picked the best items out of these and opened **Kiliwatch** in the mid-1990s. From this first shop he then developed a vintage clothes chain with Kilimarket shops in Lyon, Rennes, and Aix, among other cities, twenty-eight franchise shops in Tokyo, and a wholesale business in Rouen.

Kiliwatch is one of the bigger secondhand shops in Paris. The space covers more than 6,500 square feet with both old and new clothes. The vintage section is well stocked, with over 15,000 garments and accessories of all kinds. New items are added every week, and clothes are sourced from all over Europe and America. They cover the period from 1940 to the 1980s, but the emphasis is on clothes from the 1960s, 1970s, and 1980s. The selection is based on style rather than designer names, but there are still a fair amount of designer labels in the shop. The section devoted to secondhand clothes is divided into women's wear, menswear, sportswear, and military clothes. Selections follow trends and seasons. Some price examples: T-shirts €18–19, skirts €39, men's shirts €39, Burberry trench coats €130, and Hermès shawls €122.

Break

Rue Montorgueil
A vibrant pedestrian market street where you can find almost everything from the kingdom of French food. At number 51 you'll find Patisserie Stohrer, a lovely pastry shop *à l'ancienne.*
M° Sentier or Etienne Marcel

64, rue Tiquetonne, 75002 Paris
Monday 2 P.M.–7 P.M. / Tuesday–Saturday 11 A.M.–7:30 P.M.
T +33 1 42 21 17 37 / www.kiliwatch.fr
M° Etienne Marcel

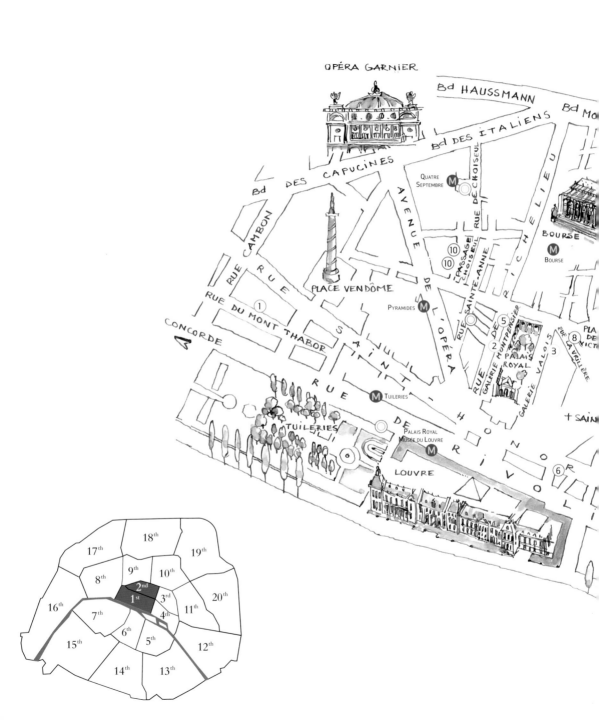

OPÉRA GARNIER

Bd HAUSSMANN

Bd Mo

Bd DES ITALIENS

Bd DES CAPUCINES

Quatre
Septembre Ⓜ

RUE DE CHOISEUL

RICHELIEU

BOURSE

Bd

RUE CAMBON

RUE

PLACE VENDÔME

AVENUE DE L'OPÉRA

PASSAGE CHOISEUL

RUE SAINTE-ANNE

Ⓜ BOURSE
Bourse

⑩
⑩

CONCORDE

RUE DU MONT THABOR

①

SAINT-

Pyramides Ⓜ

RUE DE

⑤
PALAIS
ROYAL

GALERIE MONTPENSIER

RUE DE LA VRILLIÈRE

⑧

PLA
DE
VICT

PLA

RUE

DE

Ⓜ Tuileries

HONO

GALERIE VALOIS

✝ SAIN

TUILERIES

Palais Royal
Musée du Louvre
Ⓜ

RIV

LOUVRE

⑥

O

R
I
V
O
L
I

18th

17th
9th
10th
19th

8th

2nd
1st
3rd
11th
20th

16th
7th
4th

6th
5th
12th

15th

14th
13th

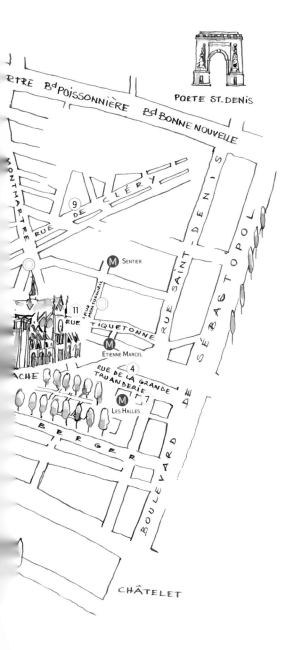

1st & 2nd
arrondissements

Shops

1. Neila Vintage & Design
2. Didier Ludot
3. La Petite Robe Noire
4. Iglaïne
5. Gabrielle Geppert
6. Création & Diffusion Rag
7. Son & Image
8. Fr/Jp Design & Vintage
9. Oldies
10. Vintage 39-41 & 51-53
11. Kiliwatch

Breaks

- La Bocca
- Higuma
- Ultramod
- Musée de la Mode et du Textile
- Rue Montorgueil

3rd

arrondissement

17th
18th
19th
8th
9th
10th
16th
2nd
1st
3rd
20th
4th
11th
7th
6th
5th
15th
12th
14th
13th

Yukiko

Yukiko opened this shop, full of feminine personality, in 2001. Her selection is small but carefully chosen. She loves the 1930s, but her shop carries women's clothes and matching accessories from all the decades of the twentieth century. Dior and Yves Saint Laurent are her favorite designers, but otherwise it is style rather than labels that determines her choices. She also has a number of lovely shoes and accessories, all in excellent condition. Prices start at €5 and reach €3,000 for certain rarities, but most are in the €50–150 range. Yukiko now also sells her own line of clothes, which are designed in the same feminine spirit that characterizes her vintage collection.

Break

Le Café Suédois
Homemade pies, soups, and Swedish cinnamon rolls, at reasonable prices and served in a historic setting at the Swedish Cultural Institute. When the weather permits, food is served in the courtyard. Exhibitions at the Institute are open to the public for free.
11, rue Payenne, 75003 Paris
Tuesday–Sunday noon–6 P.M.
T +33 1 44 78 80 11
M° Saint-Paul

97, rue Vieille du Temple, 75003 Paris
Monday–Saturday 11 A.M.–7 P.M.
T +33 1 42 71 13 41
www.yukiko-paris.com or www.vintage-paris.com
M° Saint-Sébastien Froissart

Marie Louise de Monterey

Australian Maria Vryzakis opened her shop at the end of February 2007, after living in Paris for four years. She worked as a costume designer and stage manager in her home country. When she arrived in France she began buying vintage clothes as inspiration material for a designer in New York. Maria has a yen for clothes from the 1920s and 1940s, and has built up a feminine and romantic collection of women's and children's clothes from those periods. Other decades get a look-in as well, but most items are from the 1920s and 1940s. Her collection is well arranged and in good condition. She also has a large number of shoes, and in one of the rooms is a collection by the American Lyell label, whose clothes are inspired by vintage. Prices range from €40 to €300 for women's wear; children's clothes sell for between €15 and €150. Shoes are between €20 and €150.

1, rue Charles-François Dupuis, 75003 Paris
Tuesday–Saturday noon–7 P.M.
T +33 1 48 04 83 88 or +33 6 73 87 69 46
www.marielouisedemonterey.com
M° Temple

Break

Andy Wahloo
A laid-back bar with good drinks and music. Also serves small Moroccan dishes. When the weather is clement, guests can sit in the courtyard.
69, rue des Gravilliers, 75003 Paris
Tuesday–Saturday 5 P.M.–2 A.M.
T +33 1 42 71 20 38
M° Arts et Métiers

La Jolie Garde-Robe

With just over two and a half years in existence, Marie Rouche's shop is one of the most recent on the Paris vintage scene. She specializes in women's wear and accessories dating from 1900 to the glamorous 1980s. The majority of the items are from the 1950s and 1960s. Marie's love affair with vintage clothing began—as it did for many of the other shopowners—with private collecting. When her wardrobe became too small and her passion too great, she decided to open a shop. There are about four hundred garments and accessories in her 645-square-foot shop. Designer labels include Celine, Courrèges, Pierre Cardin, and Hermès. Everything is in excellent condition. Clothes prices start at €20–30. The most expensive items are haute couture designs costing around €800—the current leader is an 1980s party dress by French designer Loris Azzaro. Shoes cost anywhere from €40 to €300. Marie's personal favorite is one of her own Courrèges dresses from the 1960s, now for sale.

She also has a sizable stock that includes clothes for men and children, textiles, and a fair amount of jewelry, including a fabulous bracelet by Line Vautrin. Visits to the warehouse are strictly by appointment.

Break

Le Marché des Enfants Rouges
Food is served along the two sides of the market. A place full of smells, colors, and good food at reasonable prices.
39, rue de Bretagne, 75003 Paris
Tuesday–Thursday 9 A.M. –2 P.M. / 4 P.M–8 P.M.
Friday–Saturday 9 A.M.–8 P.M.
Sunday 9 A.M. –2 P.M.
T +33 1 42 77 55 05
M° Filles du Calvaire or Temple

15, rue Commines, 75003 Paris
Tuesday–Saturday 2 P.M.–8 P.M.
T +33 1 42 72 13 90 or +33 6 80 91 33 55
M° Filles du Calvaire

Chez Dentelles

This is quite possibly the smallest shop in Paris. It is certainly the smallest shop in this guide. A tiny, romantic hole in the wall, it is filled with lace, textile flowers, fabric, bijoux fantaisie (novelty jewelry), dresses, and blouses for women of all sizes and shapes. While working as a designer in Japan, the owner, Shigeko, travelled to France and fell in love with handmade lace. She began to collect lace from Alençon, Valenciennes, and Argenton-sur-Creuse. This passion eventually led her to open her small shop. That was twenty years ago. Shigeko stocks treasures dating from the turn of the last century until the 1960s, but most items are from between 1900 and 1930. Prices start at €10. A gorgeous dress from the early twentieth century will set you back €400.

16, rue Rambuteau, 75003 Paris
Tuesday–Friday 11 A.M.–1 P.M. / 2:30 P.M.–7 P.M.
Saturday noon–6 P.M.
T +33 1 42 74 02 51
M° Rambuteau

La Belle Epoque

La Belle Epoque specializes in women's clothes dating from 1900 to the 1970s. The shop's display consists of exactly five hundred items, all carefully chosen and in good condition. In the atelier behind the shop is the haute couture wardrobe, for those looking for something extra special. The shop receives fifty new items every week. After several years at the Clignancourt flea market, Philippe opened his shop at this location in 1996.

"For me, every woman is unique, and through vintage she can express her originality." Philippe is happy to help anyone who needs advice on her evening outfit.

Dresses sell for €50–80, coats for around €150, and accessories for €30–50. Designer garments cost €200–500. A yellow 1960s coat by Philippe Venet is €250, and a Pucci poplin dress has the same price tag. A typical Leonard dress is €200.

10, rue de Poitou, 75003 Paris
Tuesday–Saturday 1:30 P.M.–6:30 P.M. or by appointment
T +33 6 80 77 71 32
M° Saint-Sébastien Froissart

BIJOUX
ANCIENS

La Licorne

For over thirty years, Madame Crochet has sold jewelry from the remaining stock from the family-owned factory R. Petit & Compagnie, located nearby on rue des Francs Bourgeois. Jewelry was manufactured there from 1898 until 1975, when the factory was closed down. It was a modest operation employing about fifteen workers.

The remaining stock seems like a well that never runs dry. Madame Crochet's shop is filled floor to ceiling with all manners of jewelry: black jet necklaces, colorful Galalith necklaces, glittering Swarovski earrings, and futuristic 1970s creations. All bijou styles from the beginning of the twentieth century to the 1970s are represented. Madame Crochet herself is particularly fond of 1930s designs. Prices range from €9 for a child's ring to €300 for gems from the first decades of the twentieth century.

38, rue de Sévigné, 75003 Paris
Every day 1:30 P.M.–7 P.M.
T +33 1 48 87 84 43
M° Saint-Paul

Break

Le Petit Dakar
Traditional food from Senegal, including Yassa and other dishes cooked according to recipes of Senegalese singer Youssou N'Dour's mother.
6, rue Elzévir, 75003 Paris
Tuesday–Saturday 8 P.M.–11 P.M.
T +33 1 44 59 34 74
M° Saint-Paul

Studio W

William Moricet used to run the vintage shop **Lulu de Berlu** on rue Oberkampf together with his friend Katja Rosenberg, but now he has branched out on his own. He focuses mainly on women's accessories dating from 1920 to 1980, but also stocks a small selection of clothes. His predilection for elegant, severe lines—or "sexychic," as he calls the style—is reflected in his collection. Even if quite a few exclusive designers are represented, style and quality are the main determinants of William's choices. Prices for bags range from €50 to €700. William has a soft spot for the design and needlework of bags made by the French designer Fernande Desgranges, as well as the Delvaux label from Belgium. In shoes, François Villon, Maud Frizon, and Charles Jourdan get a favorable rating, but his personal favorite is a pair of exquisite 1920s shoes in gold. Shoes and boots sell for €80–250. William also has a fine collection of jewelry, a current favorite of which is a marvelous gold-plated bronze necklace by Line Vautrin.

Break

Wéber Métaux et Plastiques
For lovers of traditional ironmongers, this is a mecca in Paris. You'll find every type of metal you can think of, including nonferrous and alloys.
9, rue du Poitou, 75003 Paris
Monday–Friday 8:30 A.M.–5:30 P.M.
T +33 1 42 71 23 45
M° Saint-Sébastien Froissart

6, rue du Pont aux Choux, 75003 Paris
Tuesday–Saturday 2 P.M.–7:30 P.M. and Monday by appointment
T +33 1 44 78 05 02 or +33 6 10 66 14 66
studio.w@free.fr
M° Saint-Sébastien Froissart

Planète 70

As the name suggests, this shop specializes in the 1970s, though the odd garment is older (from 1930 on) or younger. Saraydar opened **Planète 70** in 1992 and it has not been closed a single day since then. The shop extends over two well-filled floors and provide both men and women with clothes, accessories, and wigs. There are many students among the customers, as well as people planning 1970s-themed parties. Prices start at €5; a 1970s dress sells for €25–35, while the most expensive items are fur coats costing up to €450.

147, rue Saint-Martin, 75003 Paris
Every day 11:30 A.M.–7:30 P.M.
T +33 1 48 04 33 96
M° Rambuteau

Olga

Olivier Gampel opened his shop in the summer of 2003, and his was the first in Paris to mix new design with vintage. At first he matched clothes from labels such as Erotokritos, Cacharel, and Les Prairies de Paris with vintage accessories, but now the shop has expanded and the vintage selection has been given its own small room. Olivier has also added a small selection of vintage clothes to the accessories—all of which he found at markets all over France. The period covered is from the 1960s until the 1980s, and there are only women's items.

All shoes cost €50–70 whether they are designer shoes or not; boots cost €80–100. Chanel bags sell for €250–400. Dresses cost €60. The vintage selection is replenished every two weeks.

45, rue de Turenne, 75003 Paris
Tuesday–Saturday 11:30 A.M.–7:30 P.M.
Sunday–Monday 2:30 P.M.–7:30 P.M.
T +33 1 42 72 44 92 / olgashop@hotmail.com
M° Saint-Sébastien Froissart

Pretty Box

Sarah Cacoub opened her vintage-stuffed treasure chest in 2005. Her first shop was in passage de Choiseul, but in the summer of 2007, she moved to the present location. Secondhand shops have been a part of her life since childhood. In the early 1970s, her parents opened the first secondhand shop, Ali Baba's Cave, in Abidjan, Ivory Coast. Sarah herself has spent much of her life seeking out old pearls, and she has a soft spot for 1980s design. The 270-square-foot shop contains women's wear and accessories dating from the 1930s to the 1980s. In order to keep pace with the times, she insists that items she selects feel contemporary. No museum objects here. Clothes and accessories are sourced from all over Europe. For the 2006–2007 winter season, she bought enormous amounts of boots, and she sold 1,200 pairs in a couple of month! Prices are reasonable, with sunglasses and basic tops selling for as little as €10. Boots cost €40–120. The most expensive items are 1930s clothes and designer dresses, selling for €90–120.

46, rue de Saintonge, 75003 Paris
Monday–Saturday 11 A.M.–7 P.M.
T +33 1 48 04 81 71
M° Filles du Calvaire

3rd

arrondissement

Shops

1. Yukiko
2. Marie Louise de Monterey
3. La Jolie Garde-Robe
4. Chez Dentelles
5. La Belle Epoque
6. La Licorne
7. Studio W
8. Planète 70
9. Olga
10. Pretty Box

Breaks

◎ Le Petit Dakar
◎ Le Café Suédois
◎ Andy Wahloo
◎ Le Marché des Enfants Rouges
○ Wéber Métaux et Plastiques

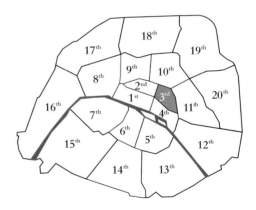

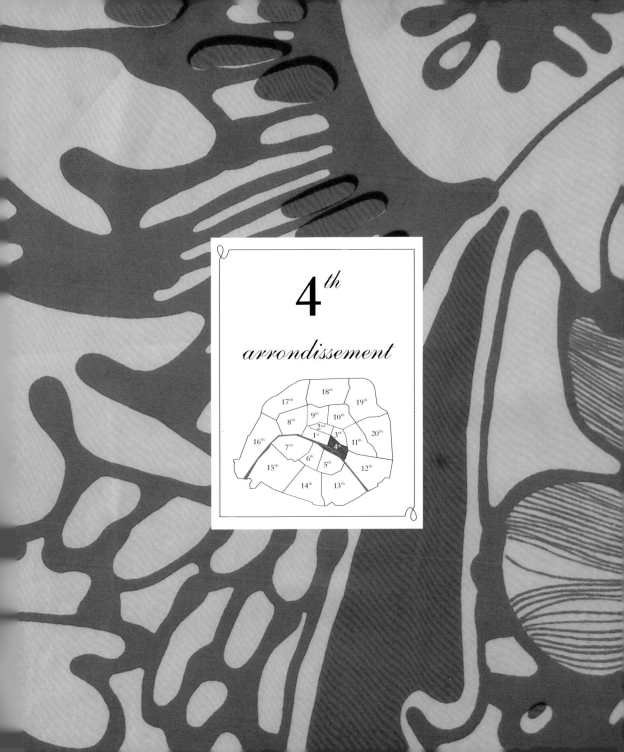

4th

arrondissement

Mamz'Elle Swing

Mamz'Elle Swing's passion has always been vintage, or retro as she calls it. She loves the 1940s and the 1950s, but sells clothes from all the decades of the twentieth century in her small shop. The selection is manageable and well planned, and continuously renewed. Most items are for women, but the odd menswear item can also be found. The clothes come from France, Britain, Germany, and Austria. For professionals, she has a warehouse outside Paris, open only by appointment. The shop opened in 1996, and customers are mostly from the worlds of fashion, advertising, film, and theatre—though many tourists find their way here as well. Prices are reasonable, varying between €10 and €400. Mamz'Elle also has a good website for those who prefer to shop online.

35 bis, rue du Roi de Sicile, 75004 Paris
Monday–Saturday 2 P.M.–7 P.M.
T +33 1 48 87 04 06 / www.mamzelleswing.fr
M° Saint-Paul

Break

L'Osteria
A very good, small Italian restaurant with wonderful dishes. It isn't visible from the street, so don't forget the address—and book a table!
10, rue de Sévigné, 75004 Paris
Tuesday–Friday noon–2:30 P.M. / 8 P.M.–10:30 P.M.
Monday 8 P.M.–10:30 P.M.
T +33 1 42 71 37 08
M° Saint-Paul

Free P Star

Mamad Ali Pour has had his well-filled shop for just over ten years. He specializes in 1950s–1980s fripes, which he sells at good prices. Most of the clothes are from Europe, as he finds US sizes difficult. Turnover in the shop is fast; new items are delivered three days a week. During the winter months, Mamad specializes in fur coats. These cost between €40 and €450, depending on quality and style. The cheapest accessories are belts selling for €3. In the summer, Mamad removes the fur coats and fills his shop with dresses, blouses, and shirts from the era. He has a second shop, **Fripes Star** (see pages 72–73), not far from here.

8, rue Sainte Croix de la Bretonnerie, 75004 Paris
Monday–Saturday noon–11 P.M.
Sunday 2 P.M.–11 P.M.
T +33 1 42 76 03 72
M° Hôtel de Ville

Sélima Optique

If you are looking for vintage sunglasses and frames from 1950 to 1990, you've come to the right place when you cross **Sélima Optique**'s threshold. Since the early 1990s, Aïda and her sister Sélima have hunted for interesting and fashionable sunglasses in the United States, Japan, France, and Italy. The sisters have become real aces at finding good designer frames. Aïda's current favorites are a pair of unused Persols from the 1960s, with flexible earpieces—which were also Steve McQueen's favorite shades. But there are also French motorcycle goggles from the 1950s, a collection of Alain Mikli's various 1980s models, American so-called Pantos from the 1950s and 1960s, haute couture frames from the 1970s by Yves Saint Laurent, Leonard, Dior, Gucci, and others, glamorous Swarovski-covered sunglasses by Jean-Louis Scherrer, and frames by the German cult brand Cazal. Prices are between €160 and €430. If you're looking for a particular model, you can contact Aïda and she will find a pair for you.

Break

Au Rendez-vous des Amis
A small, pleasant French restaurant that is open from noon until 2 AM!
10, rue Sainte-Croix de la Bretonnerie, 75003 Paris
Every day 11 A.M.–2 A.M.
They serve food from noon–midnight
T +33 1 42 72 05 99
M° Saint-Paul or Hôtel de Ville

46, rue Vieille du Temple, 75004 Paris
Tuesday–Saturday 11 A.M.–7:30 P.M.
Sunday–Monday 2 P.M.–7:30 P.M.
T +33 1 48 04 38 55
M° Saint-Paul or Hôtel de Ville

Vintage Désir

Medad opened his business here in July 2006. He has worked in the trade for thirty years; before he came here, he had a shop in Saint-Ouen. His shop has little in common with what he was doing at the flea market, though. Here he has a wide selection of women's and menswear from the 1960s, 1970s, and 1980s. Medad wants to offer a timely selection, so follows current styles and trends. He is not very impressed by designer labels, and is looking for style and craftsmanship. Price plays its part in this, too; Medad wants to keep them low. They start at €5 and reach €250 for some furs. Medad does a lot of his buying at auctions in Britain and America. All items are washed and mended before they are displayed.

32, rue des Rosiers, 75004 Paris
Every day from 11 A.M.–10 P.M.
T +33 1 40 27 04 98
M° Saint-Paul

A l'Elégance d'Autrefois

Claudio proves that a hole in the wall can house more than ten thousand objects—all it takes is a bit of organization. He opened his small shop six years ago. Before that he had his stand at various *brocantes* (flea markets) around Paris. His main specialities are shoes and accessories from the 1920s to the 1960s. Claudio has concentrated on "urban chic," so anyone looking for a more rustic style should seek elsewhere. This is a repository of elegant urban items from the past, for sale or rent. All the shoes, bags, gloves, and clothes are carefully restored and cleaned before they are put on display. Order reigns supreme at Claudio's—shoes are cleverly arranged by year and size. A pair of shoes sells for €60 to €400. Clothes are kept upstairs.

5, rue du Pas de la Mule, 75004 Paris
Tuesday–Sunday 3 P.M.–8 P.M.
T +33 1 48 87 78 84
M° Chemin Vert

Fuchsia Dentelle

The shop has been here for twenty years, but Elise only took it over at the turn of the millennium. Her romantic 280 square feet are stuffed full of lace, dresses and blouses for young and old, silk lingerie, fabric, embroidery, ribbons of all kinds, and other accessories. These treasures are from the end of the nineteenth century and up until the 1950s. Under a canopy of the most fabulous evening dresses, you can browse this lace-lined treasure chest. The selection is French. Dresses sell for €100–400, children's dresses for €60–300, and slips made of silk and lace for €85–300. Prices for various little ribbons and bits of lace start at €2–3. The most expensive items are hand-worked linen bedspreads, which can cost up to €800.

Corner of rue de l'Ave Maria and rue Saint-Paul, 75004 Paris
Tuesday–Sunday 12:30 P.M.–7 P.M.
T +33 1 48 04 75 61
M° Sully Morland, Saint-Paul, or Pont Marie

Break

Annick Goutal
A genuine Parisian perfume shop for lovers of sweet fragrances. The perfumery was created by the sister of Bonpoint founder, Marie-France Cohen, Annick Goutal, and is now run by her daughter Camille Goutal.
3 bis, rue des Rosiers, 75003 Paris
Monday–Saturday 10 A.M.–1:30 P.M. / 2:30 P.M.–7 P.M.
T +33 1 48 87 80 11
M° Saint-Paul

Francine

Francine has had this shop for more than twenty-five years. Visits are by appointment only. She has two other shops at the Marché Vernaison in Saint-Ouen's flea market (see pages 184–185), and they are open on Saturdays, Sundays, and Mondays. Francine's background is in design, and she began collecting *linge de maison* (linen) and children's clothes for inspiration. Her main specialities are antique textiles and linge de maison, but she also has a lot of clothes and accessories from the 1870s to the 1940s. For more information and examples, see the entry on her shops in Saint-Ouen.

Break

Izraël
A haven for lovers of spices and seeds, gastronomy, and exotic products.
30, rue François Miron, 75004 Paris
Monday–Saturday 11 A.M.–1 P.M. / 2 P.M.–7 P.M.
T +33 1 42 72 66 23
M° Saint-Paul or Hôtel de Ville

5, rue de l'Ave Maria, 75004 Paris
By appointment only
T +33 6 07 41 99 01
M° Sully Morland, Saint-Paul, or Pont Marie

Vertiges

Aldo was the first to open in this area by the cultural center, back in 1984. He sticks to the notion that his shop is a traditional *friperie* (secondhand shop). The main selection is clothes from the 1960s to the 1980s, but if you are lucky you can also find older clothes and theatre costumes here. The shop's 860 square feet are pretty full, and just as in many other friperies, everything is carefully sorted according to genre. Lacoste T-shirts, flowery skirts and dresses, corduroy and velvet blazers, shirts, kimonos, military jackets, and trench coats are some of the categories. Menswear and women's wear are equally represented. Prices are low and turnover is high. The lowest set prices are €5, but you can often get a quantity discount—if you buy three items priced at €5, you only pay €10. The sought-after *cycliste* (motorcyclist) and *chantier de jeunesse* (Resistance fighters) leather jackets are more expensive, selling for between €150 and €400.

85, rue Saint-Martin, 75004 Paris
Monday–Saturday 10:30 A.M.–7:30 P.M.
Sunday noon–7:30 P.M.
T +33 1 48 87 34 64
M° Rambuteau

Le Photon des Vosges

In René Ohana's shop, you'll find spectacle frames from the nineteenth century until 1990s. He is no designer fan—instead he looks for the craftsmanship that he says you rarely find in frames made after the 1980s. And his selection really does include all sorts of frames: the famous "le Corbusier" goggles from the early twentieth century, clever silver and gold frames from the early nineteenth century, and any number of sunglasses from the whole twentieth century. Prices start at €100. A pair of silver frames from 1810 costs between €1,000 and 2,000. A pair of gold frames from the 1930s will set you back around €2,000. Vintage sunglasses sell for €150–250.

9, rue du Pas de la Mule, 75004 Paris
Tuesday–Saturday 10:30 A.M.–2 P.M. / 3 P.M.–7 P.M.
Sunday–Monday 3 P.M.–7 P.M.
T +33 1 42 77 45 22
M° Chemin Vert

Fripes Star

In March 2007, **Free P Star** (see pages 60–61) opened its second shop here. This one is bigger, and just as well filled as its parent shop. Clothes are hung very close together, and there are masses of items to choose from for both women and men. Patience is required. The period covered here is from the 1950s to the 1980s. Prices are the same as in the parent shop; the only difference is really that there's more items here.

61, rue de la Verrerie, 75004 Paris
Monday–Saturday 11 A.M.–10 P.M. / Sunday 3 P.M.–10 P.M.
T +33 1 42 78 00 76
M° Hôtel de Ville

FRIPES STAR

FREE'P'STAR

1962

Rag

This shop is immediately next door to **Vertiges** and is a branch of the **Rag** on rue Saint-Honoré. The period covered is the same as in **Création & Diffusion Rag**, but the selection, quality, and price levels of the two shops are different. Designer clothes are not the priority here, but rather a broad, seasonal selection. Examples include ladies' leopard-patterned coats, trench coats, and French sailor jerseys during autumn; and light dresses, kimono seconds, patterned shirts, and blouses in the spring. And it's cheap! Prices start at €5, and you can often a get a discount if you buy three of the same items.

83, rue Saint-Martin, 75004 Paris
Monday–Saturday 10 A.M.–8 P.M. / Sunday noon–8 P.M.
T +33 1 48 87 34 64
M° Rambuteau

LOUVRE

RAMBUTEAU
M

CENTRE POMPIDOU

8
11

CHÂTELET

Bd DE SÉBASTOPOL

RUE SAINT-MARTIN

RUE ST-MARTIN

RUE DE LA VERRERIE

RUE BEAUBOURG

RUE RAMBUTEAU

RUE DU TEMPLE

RUE

RUE DES ARCHIVES

R. STE-CROIX DE LA BRETONNERIE

R. DES FRANCS

DU TEMPLE

10
1

2
3

R. VIEILLE

RUE DES ROSIERS

4

HÔTEL DE VILLE
M

HÔTEL DE VILLE

DE

RIVOLI

R. DU ROI DE SICILE

RUE MALHER

RUE DE SÉ

QUAI DE CONTI

PONT NEUF

QUAI DES GRANDS AUGUSTINS

PT AU CHANGE

ÎLE DE LA CITÉ

PT ST-MICHEL

PETIT PONT

† NOTRE DAME

QUAI ST-MICHEL

QUAI DE MONTEBELLO

QUAI DE L'HÔTEL DE VILLE

R. FRANÇOIS MIRON

Saint-Paul
M

† ST-PAUL

7
6

R. AVE MARIA

RUE SAINT

SUL MORL
M

ÎLE SAINT-LOUIS

PONT MARIE
M

Q. DES CÉLESTINS

QUAI DE LA TOURNELLE

PONT DE SULLY

QUAI SAINT-BERNARD

17th
18th
19th
8th
9th
10th
2nd
1st
3rd
16th
7th
11th
20th
4th
6th
15th
5th
12th
14th
13th

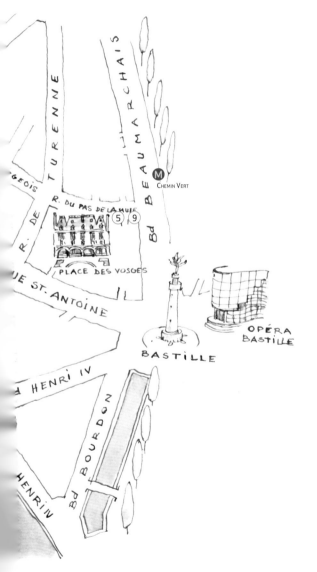

RÉPUBLIQUE

PLACE DES VOSGES

BASTILLE

OPÉRA BASTILLE

4th arrondissement

Shops

① Mamz'Elle Swing
② Free P Star
③ Sélima Optique
④ Vintage Désir
⑤ A l'Elégance d'Autrefois
⑥ Fuchsia Dentelle
⑦ Francine
⑧ Vertiges
⑨ Le Photon des Vosges
⑩ Fripes Star
⑪ Rag

Breaks

◎ Au Rendez-vous des Amis
◎ L'Osteria
◎ Izraël
◎ Annick Goutal

6th, 7th, 14th & 15th

arrondissements

Aurélie Antiquaire

Aurélie has had her small shop since the 1990s, and specializes in designer items, hats, and bijoux fantaisie. The time period covered extends from the turn of the previous century to the 1970s. For a while Aurélie had a great demand for Art Deco, but now her focus is on accessories from 1940 to 1970. She has an enormous amount of jewelry made from Galalith, which was a precursor to Bakelite. Otherwise, designer labels such as Chanel and Hermès are rated highly here. For collectors of perfume flacons, there's a whole glass-fronted case full of them. Prices vary between €60 and €700.

12, rue de l'Echaudé, 75006 Paris
Monday–Saturday 2:30 P.M.–7 P.M.
T +33 1 46 33 59 41
M° Mabillon or Saint-Germain des Prés

Break

Bonpoint
Marie-France Cohen's latest flagship store for her luxurious children's clothes and accessories. An enormous temple for children and parents designed by the French architect François Murracciole. A little extra is the café for the tired ones that need a bit of energy for the shopping tour.
Hôtel de Brancas,
6, rue de Tournon, 75006 Paris
Monday–Saturday 10 A.M.–7 P.M.
T +33 1 40 51 98 20
M° Odéon

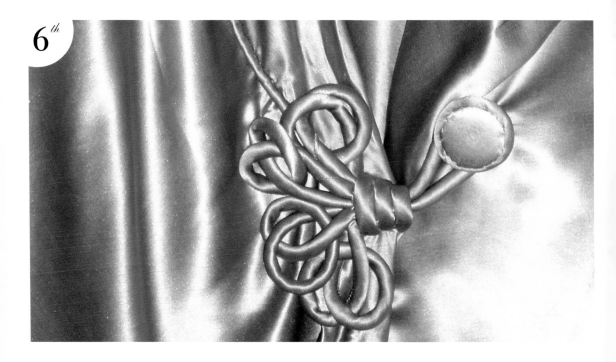

Ragtime

Françoise Auguet opened her first secondhand shop in 1975, in the first arrondissement. In 1999, she moved to this location. With over thirty years in the business, she has become a real connoisseur of vintage clothes and fabrics. It was Françoise who compiled and wrote the catalogue that the Drouot-Richelieu auction house produced for the sale of Paul and Denise Poiret's collection in May 2005. The catalogue immediately became an invaluable work of reference.

Her selection in the shop covers clothes from throughout the twentieth century, and also includes some nineteenth-century creations. Her own favorite period is the 1930s, which she says brings out femininity with simplicity and elegance. She deals mainly in women's clothes, but the odd menswear item can also be found in her selection. The shop's 485 square feet are filled with around eight hundred garments, and each week brings new additions. Most of the clothes she sells are French, and made in France, because Françoise believes that French dressmakers have a finesse rarely found anywhere else. Prices vary widely—a €100 dress can be hung next to a coat priced at €10,000. Prices for certain accessories start at €20.

23, rue de l'Echaudé, 75006 Paris
Monday–Saturday 2:30 P.M.–7:30 P.M.
T +33 1 56 24 00 36 or +33 6 16 10 35 35
francoise.auguet@noos.fr
M° Mabillon or Saint-Germain des Prés

Breaks

Le Café de Flore
An institution for artists and intellectuals. The café opened in the late nineteenth century. It was the favorite hangout for people such as Apollinaire, André Breton, Jean-Paul Sartre, Simone de Beauvoir, Boris Vian, and Juliette Greco.
172, boulevard Saint-Germain, 75006 Paris
Every day 7:30 A.M.–1:30 A.M.
T +33 1 45 48 55 26
M° Saint-Germain des Prés

Ladurée
The famous pastry shop and teahouse was founded by the Ladurée family in 1862. They make the best macaroons in Paris!
21, rue Bonaparte, 75006 Paris
Monday–Saturday 8:30 A.M.–7:30 P.M.
Sunday 10:30 A.M.–7:30 P.M.
T +33 1 44 07 64 87
M° Saint-Germain des Prés

Les Trois Marches de Catherine B.

Catherine opened her first shop here in 1994; today she has two. One is small but well filled with accessories by Hermès and Chanel, including sought-after Birkin and Kelly bags and a vast collection of scarves, jewelery, belts, perfume bottles, and other accessories. Her other shop is bigger and full of clothes by the above designers and Louis Vuitton. The period covered extends from the 1940s to the present. Everything is original and in mint condition. A Monaco bag (predecessor of the popular Kelly bag) from 1944 costs around €2,500, while Kelly bags sell for between €2,000 and €3,500. Chanel suits from the 1950s and 1960s are between €900 and €2,000; Hermès scarves between €150 and €300. Catherine also has a useful Web site with information about the current selection and the possibility of buying items that are in stock.

1, rue Guisarde, 75006 Paris
Monday–Saturday 10:30 A.M.–7:30 P.M.
T +33 1 43 54 74 18 or +33 6 74 98 17 25
www.catherine-b.com
M° Mabillon

La Renaissance

This shop used to be called Catherine Arigoni after its owner. Today it is run in the same spirit by Catherine's daughter, Corinne Than-Trong. Catherine Arigoni specialized in vintage haute couture. She began her career in the business at the end of the 1990s by selling one of her own haute couture dresses, an Yves Saint Laurent creation from the 1970s. One thing led to another, and over the years she collected a small but exquisite collection of French haute couture clothes and bijoux. Her particular speciality, though, was fur coats of leopard, jaguar, and ocelot. Corinne has updated the collection with clothes by Pierre Cardin. You will also find creations such as a lime green Madame Grès dress from the 1950s for €1,500; a pearl-embroidered Balmain top for €3,000; a cape from 1910 by Sœurs Callot, or a unique Schiaparelli necklace of colored glass.

Break

Le Midi Vins
A chic little local bistro that offers value for money.
83, rue du Cherche-Midi, 75006 Paris
Closed Sunday and Monday
T +33 1 45 48 33 71
M° Vaneau

14, rue de Beaune, 75007 Paris
Monday 3 P.M.–7 P.M.
Tuesday–Saturday 11 A.M.–7 P.M.
T +33 1 42 60 95 49 / www.renaissance75007.com
M° Rue du Bac

Magic Retour

If you happen to be in the area, you can drop in on Olivier Soulas' secondhand shop. It's been here for thirty-three years! He began as an interior decorator, and as such travelled around to flea markets all over France. He soon developed an interest in vintage clothes, and one thing led to another. Olivier sold mostly older items when he started out, but today they are hard to find and most often too expensive to buy when you do. So today he mainly sells clothes from the 1940s, 1950s, and 1960s. Most are for women, but he also has some men's shirts and jackets. A day dress from the period sells for around €15, but for a Charleston dress you have to be prepared to pay around €300.

Break

Rue Daguerre
Between avenue du Général Leclerc and avenue du Maine, there is rue Daguerre, a pedestrian street with a daily open-air market in a genuine Parisian setting.
M° Denfert Rochereau

36, rue de la Sablière, 75014 Paris
Tuesday–Saturday 2:30 P.M.–7:30 P.M.
M° Pernety

Doursoux

A 970-square-foot space devoted to all sorts of army clothes and accessories from the 1930s until the present, **Doursoux** has been here since 1974. There is also a catalogue-sales part of the business, located outside Paris, along with dressmaking workshops that will make older models to order and also manufacture re-releases of certain models for the shop. The clothes are sourced from France, Britain, the United States, and the former Soviet Union, among other places. The owners are particularly proud of a Japanese kamikaze pilot's outfit from the Second World War, including all the original accessories, in mint condition. It is not for sale, though. There are plenty of other things to buy, however, for both men and women. Prices for shoes are between €30 and €190, and they come in size 37 (US size 6) and up.

3, passage Alexandre, 75015 Paris
Tuesday–Saturday 10 A.M.–7:30 P.M.
T +33 1 43 27 00 97 / www.doursoux.com
M° Pasteur

RUE DU BAC

TOUR EIFFEL

INVALIDES

7th

Bd

RUE DE

R. DE VARENNE

AVENUE DE SUFFREN

BOULEVARD DE GRENELLE

RUE DE BABYLONE

DE SÉGUR

Bd GARIBALDi

AVENUE DE BRETEUIL

RUE DE SÈV

VANEAU
M

15th

RUE LECOURBE

Bd PASTEUR

RUE DE

RUE

DE

TOUR
MONTPARNASSE

RUE DE VAUGIRARD

PASTEUR
M

Bd DE VAUGIRARD

6

PASSAGE
ALEXANDRE

RUE D'ALESIA

RUE RAYMOND LOSSERAND

M
PERNETY

5

R. DE LA SABLIÈRE

RUE D'ALES

17th
18th
19th
8th
9th
10th
2nd
1st
3rd
20th
16th
7th
4th
11th
15th
6th
5th
12th
14th
13th

6th & 7th & 14th & 15th

arrondissements

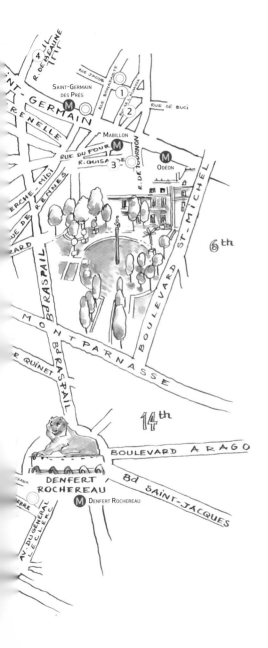

Shops

1. Aurélie Antiquaire
2. Ragtime
3. Les Trois Marches de Catherine B.
4. La Renaissance
5. Magic Retour
6. Doursoux

Breaks

◎ Bonpoint
◎ Le Café de Flore
◎ Le Midi Vins
◎ Ladurée
◎ Rue Daguerre

8th, 16th & 17th

arrondissements

Scarlett

Scarlett opened her first shop on boulevard Richard Lenoir in 1990, and dealt in clothes and accessories from the nineteenth century. Today she has changed speciality to designer goods from the twentieth century. In 1999, she opened her eponymous shop devoted to Chanel and Hermès. The period covered extends from the 1980s until the present. If you are looking for a Kelly bag or a Chanel jacket, this is the place to go. Prices for the famous Kelly bag range from €2,000 to €3,500.

10, rue Clément Marot, 75008 Paris
Monday–Friday 11 A.M.–7:30 P.M. / Saturday 2 P.M.–7 P.M.
T +33 1 56 89 03 00
M° Franklin D. Roosevelt

Break

Artcurial
An auction house situated in the impressive nineteenth-century Hôtel Dassault. It also has a gallery, a bookshop specializing in art and architecture, and a very nice café.
7, rond-point des Champs-Elysées, 75008 Paris
T +33 1 42 99 16 16 / www.artcurial.com
M° Franklin D. Roosevelt or Champs-Elysées Clemenceau

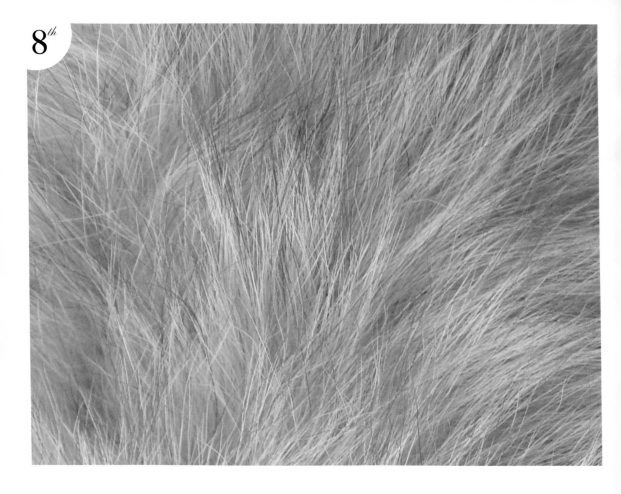

Les Antiquaires de la Mode

In 2003, Scarlett opened her second shop, just a block away from her **Scarlett** shop. Here she sells other well-known designers such as Balenciaga and Lanvin. In the early spring of 2005, she set up a showroom for vintage haute couture open by appointment only. Here she sells haute couture from the 1920s up until the present. Evening gowns by Jeanne Lanvin, Balmain, and others, all properly packaged, hang in rows. She also plans for future vintage haute couture by buying one creation from each new Dior collection. Prices start at €50, but rarities are considerably more expensive.

⌒⌒

3, rue Chambiges, 75008 Paris
Monday–Friday 11 A.M.–7:30 P.M. / Saturday 2 P.M.–7 P.M.
T +33 1 47 20 56 19
M° Franklin D. Roosevelt

Nuits de Satin

In 2004, Ghislaine Rayer opened the shop she herself had always been looking for: one devoted to vintage lingerie. During most of her life she has nurtured a passion for what women, throughout history, have worn underneath. Her interest was awakened in her teens, when she read descriptions of corsets and other small "wonders" by writers such as Flaubert and Zola. Over the years, Ghislaine has accumulated a sizable collection—more than ten thousand garments—and become something of an expert in the area. Her shop is a real gold mine for anyone interested in unused or very slightly used vintage lingerie. On the shop's shelves are one thousand carefully chosen underthings. The period covered by the lingerie extends from 1900 to the 1960s.

Before 1930, there was no manufacturing of lingerie to speak of. Instead women made their own. The items from this period in Ghislaine's collection are mostly from *trousseaux* (wedding undergarments). They are meticulously and exquisitely embroidered, and have only been used on one or a few special occasions.

The lingerie from 1940–60 is all from various warehouses around France, and none of it has ever been used—often the original label is still intact, or the garment is still neatly wrapped in its original packaging. A slip from the 1930s costs €150, babydoll slips from the 1960s sell for around €60, and for *guêpières* (garters) from the 1950s and 1960s, Ghislaine charges around €180.

In January 2006, Ghislaine launched her own collection, in which she has created lingerie after vintage models but with modern comfort. Her motto is that you should be as elegant underneath as you are on top.

5, rue Jean Bologne, 75016 Paris,
Monday–Friday 11:30 A.M.–6 P.M.
T +33 1 45 27 27 45 / www.nuitsdesatin.com
Mᵒ la Muette or Passy

Stéphane

Have a weakness for Savile Row suits, Harris Tweed jackets, or Francesco Smalto's 1970s wardrobe? Or are you dreaming of a pair of Oxfords from Crockett & Jones, English riding boots, or a pair of double strap Monk shoes by John Lobb? In that case, head for Stéphane's. For over twenty-five years he has filled his shop with classic menswear and shoes of English quality and style. This does not mean, however, that everything has to have been made in England. It is craftsmanship, cut, and material that determines Stéphane's selection, dated from the turn of the previous century until the present. Stéphane used to have two shops in marché Paul Bert in the Saint-Ouen flea market, but has now been based here for nearly a decade. For most of his life he has also been a passionate *soulier* (cobbler), and it is thanks to this hobby that he has developed his nose for all things related to leather.

Break

Bistrot des Dames
An oasis, with a garden where you can have lunch or dinner in fair weather.
18, rue des Dames, 75017 Paris
Every day 12 P.M.-2:30 P.M. and 7 P.M.-2 A.M.
Saturday and Sunday afternoon
T +33 1 45 22 13 42
M° Place de Clichy

65, place du Docteur Félix Lobligeois, 75017 Paris
Monday–Saturday 10:30 A.M.–1 P.M. / 2:30 P.M.–7 P.M.
Closed Wednesday
T +33 1 42 26 00 14
M° Rome or La Fourche

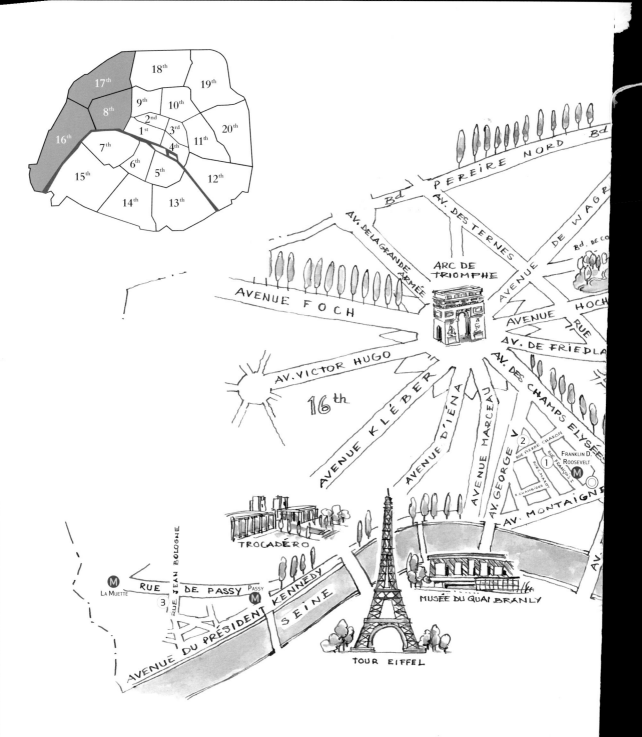

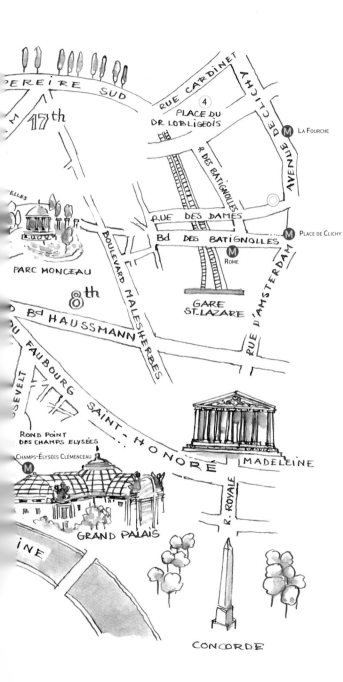

8th & 16th & 17th
arrondissements

Shops

1. Scarlett
2. Les Antiquaires de la Mode
3. Nuits de Satin
4. Stéphane

Breaks

◎ Bistrot des Dames
◎ Artcurial

9th & 10th

arrondissements

Wochdom

In a short period of time, Rudy Cohen has become something of a guru for the second generation of vintage lovers. He opened his first vintage concept store in 2003. The interior is black and severe. Here he sells clothes and accessories dating from the end of the nineteenth century to the 1990s, with the main selection focusing on the 1970s, 1980s, and 1990s. Rudy buys his clothes all over the world and when he can, he also picks up so-called dead stocks. He is meticulous about quality, and everything he sells is either unused or in mint condition. The selection includes Pierre Cardin, Dior, Celine, Ted Lapidus, and Paco Rabanne—but Rudy emphasizes that it is the style and not the label that is important. New deliveries arrive every week. Shoes sell for €50 and up, and for a black cocktail dress from the 1950s Rudy charges €150. The price range for dresses is also about €50 to €150, while men's shirts sell for around €20. And one corner of the shop is dedicated to fashion magazines and vinyl records from the era.

For the real pros, Rudy has a warehouse outside Paris, which can be visited by appointment.

72, rue Condorcet, 75009 Paris
Monday–Saturday noon–8 P.M.
T +33 1 53 21 09 72 / wochdom@hotmail.com
M° Anvers or Pigalle

Break

Musée Ary Scheffer or
Musée de la Vie Romantique
In the garden, among roses and lilies,
tea and lighter meals are served.
16, rue Chaptal, 75009 Paris
Every day except Mondays, 11:30 A.M.–5 P.M.
T +33 1 55 31 95 67
M° Blanche or Pigalle

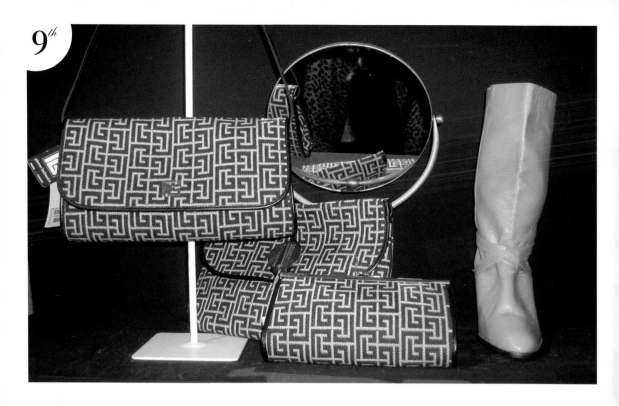

Chezel

Guerrisol's former longtime style oracles, brothers Riad and Trabelsi, opened their own shop in October 2005. They carry on in the spirit of the celebrated "Guerrisol style." They have spent ten years rifling through piles of clothes and accessories and ferreting out old stocks all over the world. This dedicated searching has provided them with a fine collection of unused clothes and accessories, such as a set of suitcases from Balmain with the original label. Those garments that are not unused are nevertheless in good condition. And even if you can find the odd outfit from the first half of the twentieth century, the main focus is on the last three decades of the century. As the name Chezel (*chez + elle*) suggests, this a women's wardrobe—one where the brothers cheerfully mix the high and the low. A transparent 1970s raincoat with dots hangs next to a haute couture top by Loris Azzaro. A suit by Lanvin hangs next to 1980s printed T-shirts. Designer suits sell for €150 to €200. Unused patterned woollen jackets from the 1970s are between €50 and €60. The cheapest clothes are those classified as fripes.

Break

Hôtel Amour
If you're after the trendy stuff, this is the right place to hang out (or stay—book well ahead!). Everything is comme il faut: the right designers, the right clientele, and the right music.
8, rue de Navarin, 75009 Paris
T +33 1 48 78 31 80
M° Saint-Georges or Pigalle

59, rue Condorcet, 75009 Paris
Tuesday–Saturday 1 P.M.–8 P.M.
T +33 1 53 16 47 31
M° Anvers or Pigalle

Ménage à 3

Good friends Hélène Cristofani and Nathalie Benezet opened their small shop in December 2006. They have created an intimate and playful space with their own mix of vintage and new designer wear. The idea is that women should be able to find their own look for a reasonable sum. So far, 70 percent of the clothes are secondhand, but the plan is for half new, half old. It is women's wear only, with the exception of a few children's clothes. A lot of the stock is from the 1980s, with some 1970s and 1990s things as well. The new collection is made up of clothes from le Mont-Saint-Michel,

Betsey Johnson, and Ella Moss, among others. The owners aren't hung up on designers; it is style they are after—and the style is young and colorful. The shop is rearranged every week, with the hundred or so garments on display replaced by others. Behind the scenes, Hélène and Nathalie have at least five hundred items awaiting their turn. In the accessory department, they sell sunglasses, jewelery, gadgets, and bags. Prices start at €1. The most expensive items are certain dresses, which sell for €150–180, but most items cost around €50.

9, rue Clauzel, 75009 Paris
Thursday–Friday 3:30 P.M.–7:30 P.M.
Saturday 10:30 A.M.–7:30 P.M. or by appointment
T +33 1 48 78 44 80 or +33 6 77 15 71 68
www.menage-a-trois.fr
M° Saint-Georges or Pigalle

Anouchka

If Didier Ludot is the uncrowned king of vintage, Anouchka is his queen. With the same number of years in the business, but with a different approach, Anouchka has created a vintage temple for the pros. Reminiscent of the costume department of a major theatre or film studio, her collection can make the most experienced visitor feel a bit daunted. It is made up of several million garments and accessories, and is partially housed here, in a spacious turn-of-the-century apartment. The rest of the collection is stored in a warehouse. Everything is carefully sorted and accounted for according to era, designer, or genre.

Anouchka's clients include designers and stylists thirsting for inspiration and looking for something old that can be dusted off and used as a basis for a new creation.

This is no ordinary secondhand shop but a *bibliothèque vivante* (a living library), a repository of knowledge from which a serious culture-consultancy business is run, so none of the garments are actually for sale; they can only be rented. But it does happen that the occasional item is sold. The haute couture part of the collection is mainly French in origin, but there are plenty of other items to interest and inspire today's designers.

Since Anouchka both predicts and follows fashion trends, her collection is constantly being changed and renewed. Last year, for instance, Yves Saint Laurent, Ossie Clark, and 1930s styles were pulled out of storage.

6, avenue du Coq, 75009 Paris
Only by appointment, Tuesday–Saturday noon–7 P.M.
T +33 1 48 74 37 00
M° Saint-Lazare

Chic Office

Sarah Stenitz, Elise Voitey, and Alice Aladjen share a passion for fashion and clothes. Elise, with a background as a costume designer in film, felt that there was no good costume warehouse for newer designer clothes, that is, items from the 1960s and up to the present day. With her two partners she, therefore, opened this showroom where they rent out clothes for professional purposes as well as to private individuals. Visits are by appointment only.

In 2007, they were offered a small space in the antiques area surrounding the Drouot auction house. There they sell women's designer clothes spanning the same period.

The collection is not large, but it is full of stars such as Pucci, Mugler, Alaïa, and Montana. The owners are particularly fond of the 1980s.

There are also newer accessories. At the center of the space is a small display case with bijoux fantaisie. The price range is €50–2,000. A Montana leather jacket from the early 1980s sells for €1,500. A typical Mugler suit from the same period, in black suede with gold lamé studs, will set you back €2,000. An ingenious Pucci evening dress from the early 1970s is priced at €1,200, while newer bags from Celine and Gucci sell for around €150.

19, rue de la Grange Batelière, 75009 Paris
Monday–Friday 10:30 A.M.–7:30 P.M.
T +33 1 48 01 04 36
M° Richelieu Drouot or Grands Boulevards

Showroom by appointment
31, rue Saint-Lazare, 75009 Paris
T +33 1 40 26 83 59
M° Notre Dame de Lorette

Mamie

About fifteen years ago, wife and husband Brigitte and Yannick turned their passion for retro clothes and accessories into **Mamie**, one of the bigger vintage shops in Paris. It is so stuffed with clothes and accessories that you can hardly make out the pink walls. In the basement are piles of right-foot shoes, the upper floor is given over to women's clothes and the odd items of children's clothing, while the room behind the entrance is for menswear. The time period covered extends from 1900 until the 1970s. Brigitte loves the craftsmanship of older clothes, and is less interested in designer labels. Her own favorite period is between 1938 and 1948. Prices are reasonable, with dresses selling for €25 and up. For a man's suit in good condition, the couple charge around €135. Shoes sell for between €15 and €90; men's shoes are often a little pricier than women's.

73, rue de Rochechouart, 75009 Paris
Tuesday–Friday 11 A.M.–1:30 P.M. / 3 P.M.–8 P.M.
Monday and Saturday 3 P.M.–8 P.M.
T +33 1 42 82 09 98 / www.mamie-vintage.com
M° Anvers

Mamie Blue

In March 2007, **Mamie** expanded by opening a new shop, **Mamie Blue**, a few doors down the street. The 1,300-square-foot space has taken some of the storage pressure off the first shop, which was ready to burst, but it is also cutting a different profile: a vintage concept store! The business here is *relooking* and *retouches sur place*, which means you can get outfitted from tip to toe. But the look is strictly 1920s to 1960s. If you need to make any alterations, they are done in the shop. While you wait, the waist can be taken in or the trouser leg hemmed. Popular models that are no longer available can also be made to order. This is the place to go if you want something special but need it to fit like a glove. Prices for alterations go from €5 to €50 depending on what you want done. "There are so few people these days who can sew," as Brigitte explains.

69, rue de Rochechouart, 75009 Paris
Monday 2:30 P.M.–7:30 P.M.
Tuesday–Saturday 11:30 A.M.–1:30 P.M. / 3 P.M.–8 P.M.
T +33 1 42 81 10 42 / www.mamie-vintage.com
M° Anvers

Guerrisol

This is the largest of **Guerrisol**'s shops, the flea market of flea markets, the friperie of fripes. Under harsh strip lights, the patient customer can search through an enormous selection of about twenty thousand garments and come up with some real finds. Prices are low, typically ranging from €1.50 to €30. There are three other branches, one in the tenth arrondissement, one in the seventeenth, and one in the eighteenth, all with the same selection and prices.

17, boulevard Rochechouart,
75009 Paris
Every day 10 A.M.–8 P.M.
T +33 1 45 26 13 12
M° Barbès Rochechouart

45, boulevard de la Chapelle,
75010 Paris
Every day 10 A.M.–8 P.M.
M° Barbès Rochechouart

21, boulevard Barbès,
75018 Paris
Monday–Saturday 10 A.M.–8 P.M.
M° Château Rouge

19, avenue de Clichy,
75017 Paris
Monday–Saturday 10 A.M.–8 P.M.
T +33 1 40 08 03 00
M° Place de Clichy

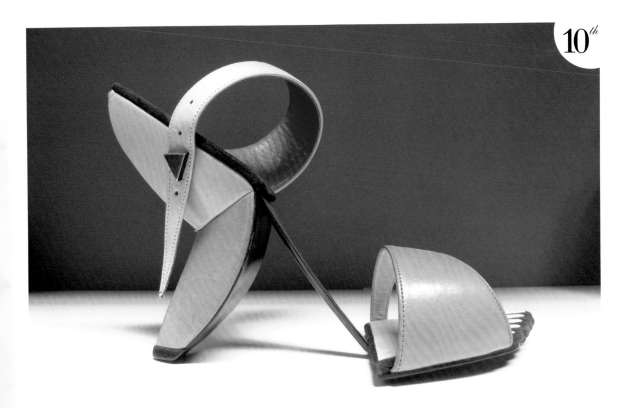

Quidam de Revel

Emmanuelle and Philippe opened their first shop in November 2000. It was an exquisite vintage gem at 24-26 rue du Poitou. In the autumn of 2007, they moved their business to the current address. They specialize in designer clothes from the period between 1920 and 1980, as well as in Scandinavian and French jewelery by famous artists from the 1930s to the 1980s. About 90 percent of the items are for women, the rest for men. Emmanuelle and Philippe buy their clothes all over the world, and their selection is colorful, of good quality and great originality. About eleven thousand garments are spread over the showroom's 2,370 square feet. Each item has been hand-picked, and the couple's individual and confident taste has given the shop its

own trademark. Emmanuelle's favorites among designers include Dior's "New Look" and Paul Poiret. Besides clothes and accessories they have a large collection of jewelry. They have collected pieces made by artists including Claude Momiron, Claude Lalanne, Line Vautrin, Michel Buffet, Georg Jensen, and Torun Bülow-Hübe. The selection of these artists' work is impressive. French Art Deco jewels and haute couture jewels are also part of their assortment.

Opening hours are limited, since the pair work mainly with costume designers, clothes designers, and stylists who rent or buy clothes or accessories. But making an appointment here is well worth the trouble. Very few items are for sale, but everything is for rent.

55, rue des Petites Ecuries, 75010 Paris
Stairway D, 1st floor, only by appointment
T +33 1 42 71 37 07 or +33 6 10 04 97 80
www.quidam-de-revel.com
M° Poissonnière, Château d'Eau, or Bonne Nouvelle

Zôa

Alexandra Fiess opened her shop here in September 2005. Her interest in vintage children's clothes developed when she was shopping for her own children in Paris flea markets. This is the first and only vintage shop wholly dedicated to children's clothes and accessories. The collection dates from the 1930s until 1980. Sizes go from 0 to 12 years. It's an international collection, as Alexandra has built up an excellent network that supplies her with gems from near and far. You can find small white embroidered romper suits, gingham dresses for the very smallest, an enchanting 1940s dress for a girl turning five, trench coats, jackets, rainwear, and much more. Baby clothes cost between €5 and €25. A green Burberry trench coat for a four-year-old sells for €125, tweed jackets for about €39. Clothes from Zôa can also be found in the children's section of Bon Marché.

Break

Hôtel du Nord
The legendary old hotel has new owners and a good restaurant with outdoor seating when the sun shines.
102, quai de Jemmapes, 75010 Paris
T +33 1 40 40 78 78
www.hoteldunord.org
M° Gare de l'Est

55, rue de Lancry, 75010 Paris
Tuesday–Saturday noon–7 P.M.
Sunday 3:30 P.M.–7 P.M.
Only open from March to September
T +33 1 44 52 01 67 / www.zoa.fr
M° Jacques Bonsergent

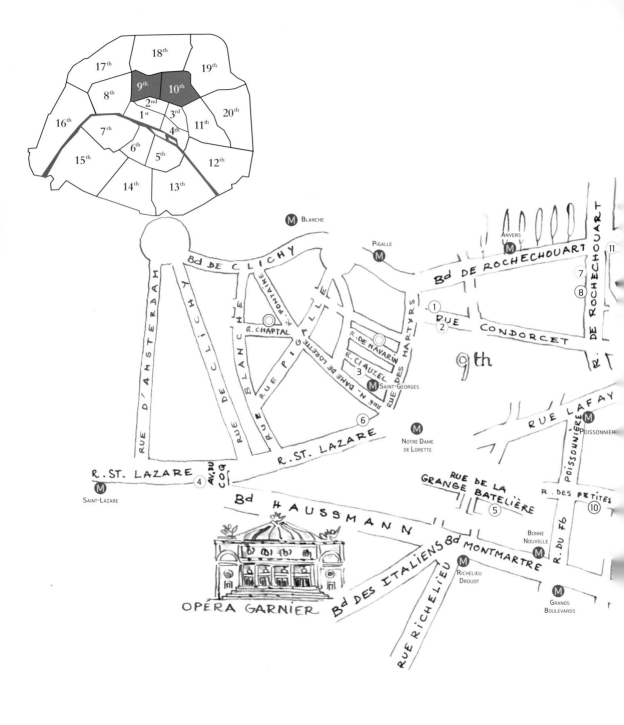

17th

18th

19th

8th 9th 10th

2nd

1st 3rd 20th

7th 4th 11th

6th

16th 5th 12th

15th

14th 13th

Ⓜ BLANCHE

PIGALLE
Ⓜ

Bd DE CLICHY

Bd DE ROCHECHOUART

ANVERS
Ⓜ

R. DE ROCHECHOUART

11

7

8

RUE D'AMSTERDAM

RUE DE CLICHY

RUE BLANCHE

RUE FONTAINE

R. CHAPTAL

RUE PIGALLE

RUE N-DAME DE LORETTE

RUE DES MARTYRS

R. DE NAVARIN

R. CLAUZEL

① ②

RUE CONDORCET

9th

3

Ⓜ SAINT-GEORGES

6

RUE LAFAY

Ⓜ POISSONNIÈR
POISSONNIÈRE

R. ST. LAZARE

Ⓜ NOTRE DAME
de LORETTE

R. ST. LAZARE

AV. DU COQ

4

Ⓜ
SAINT-LAZARE

RUE DE LA
GRANGE BATELIÈRE

R. DES PETITES

5

10

Bd HAUSSMANN

BONNE
NOUVELLE
Ⓜ

R. DU Fb

Bd DES ITALIENS Bd MONTMARTRE

RICHELIEU
DROUOT
Ⓜ

RUE RICHELIEU

GRANDS
BOULEVARDS
Ⓜ

OPÉRA GARNIER

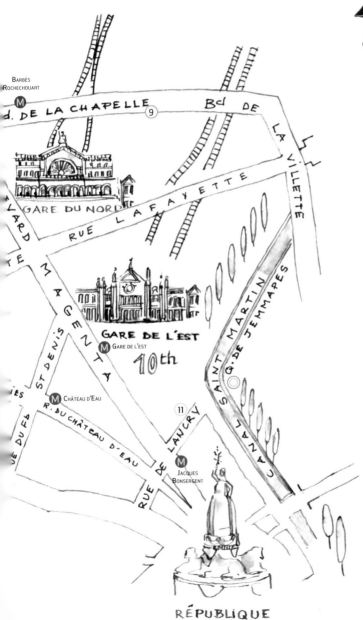

9th & 10th
arrondissements

Shops

1. Wochdom
2. Chezel
3. Ménage à 3
4. Anouchka
5. Chic Office
6. Chic Office Showroom
7. Mamie
8. Mamie Blue
9. Guerrisol
10. Quidam de Revel
11. Zôa

Breaks

◎ Hôtel du Nord
◎ Musée Ary Scheffer or Musée de la Vie Romantique
◎ Hôtel Amour

11th

arrondissement

Adöm

After a few years in the business, Mika opened his own secondhand shop in the summer of 2003. He specializes in the 1960s, 1970s, and 1980s. About two thousand garments fill his medium-sized space, arranged by type and model, e.g., Burberry trench coats, corduroy jackets, Adidas jackets, patterned skirts, striped Saint James sweaters, and so on. Mika also stocks a fairly large number of women's boots. As usual, the selection is seasonal. He used to stock more designer items, but decided to change to suit his clientele. However, you can still find Hermès scarves, and dresses and blouses by Leonard and Pucci. Prices start at €5. Shirts cost €15, Adidas jackets €35, Hermès scarves €90, and Burberry trench coats about €150. The costliest item is a Pucci dress in excellent condition, selling for €900. In spring 2007, he opened a second shop just across the street. You can't miss it!

35 and 56, rue de la Roquette, 75011 Paris
Monday–Saturday 11 A.M.–8 P.M.
Sunday 3 P.M.–8 P.M.
T +33 1 43 57 54 92 or +33 1 48 07 15 94
M° Bastille

Breaks

A la Renaissance
French brasserie and bar serving food both indoors and outdoors.
87, rue de la Roquette, 75011 Paris
Every day 8 A.M.–2 A.M.
T +33 1 43 79 83 09
M° Voltaire

Café Moderne
Serves Moroccan and French dishes at moderate prices in a pleasant setting.
19, rue Keller, 75011 Paris
Tuesday–Sunday noon–2 P.M. /
7 P.M.–midnight
T +33 1 47 00 53 62
M° Voltaire or Ledru Rollin

En Ville

Alexandra and David opened their spacious and cleanly styled vintage concept store in September 2004. They are fond of the 1960s, 1970s, and 1980s, and collaborate closely with a wholesaler where they carefully select their clothes and accessories. Everything is in top condition, and women's and men's need are equally seen to. Additionally, there are lots of matching shoes, boots, and bags to choose from. Designers are not a priority; instead it is style they are after. The large space is well filled without feeling crowded. The selection is renewed twice a month. Prices for men's sweaters are €35–70. Velvet jackets sell for €64. Dresses cost between €64 and €107; boots between €80 and €110. A pearl-strewn evening top by Oleg Cassini (Jackie Kennedy's favorite designer) will set you back €700, a Pucci dress in excellent condition between €500 and €900.

13, rue Paul Bert, 75011 Paris
Tuesday–Saturday 12:30 P.M.–8 P.M.
T +33 1 43 71 07 30
M° Faidherbe Chaligny

Breaks

Unico
An Argentinian restaurant for meat lovers, and one of the first nonsmoking restaurants in Paris.
15, rue Paul Bert, 75011 Paris
Every day except Sunday and Monday
T +33 1 43 67 68 08
M° Faidherbe Chaligny

Le Bistrot Paul Bert
Very pleasant and popular French bistro, serving good food at humane prices. Book ahead.
18, rue Paul Bert, 75011 Paris
Tuesday–Saturday noon–2 P.M. / 7:30 P.M.–11 P.M.
T +33 1 43 72 24 01
M° Faidherbe Chaligny

Vintage Clothing Paris

There is nothing ingratiating about the decoration of Brigitte Petit's shop, but a very individual and sophisticated selection of women's clothes hang from the randomly positioned clothes racks. She puts a great deal of time and effort into finding that special item for her selection. All the clothes are in top condition. There are also accessories such as shoes and bags. After just over a decade at the Saint-Ouen flea market, Brigitte opened her shop here in 2002. The time period covered extends from the beginning of the last century until the 1970s. Her own favorite period is the 1930s: silk dresses from that era sell for between €200 and €300. There is also a lot of 1960s prêt-à-porter as well as designs by Lanvin, Yves Saint Laurent, Leonard, and others. If you are looking for trousers, you'll have to look elsewhere, though. Prices start at €30. The most expensive garment currently in the shop is a striking ocelot fur costing €600.

10, rue de Crussol, 75011 Paris
Thursday–Friday noon–6:30 P.M.
Saturday 2 P.M.–6 P.M.
T +33 148 07 16 40 or +33 6 03 00 64 78
www.vintageclothingparis.com
M° Oberkampf or Filles du Calvaire

Casablanca

Najat Kas began her career as a costume designer for the screen and stage, and in a way she never left it, as she still collaborates closely with many of her former colleagues. Her shop, one of the largest in Paris, opened in 1996. It holds about twenty thousand garments for men, women, and children. Najat's specialities are casual clothes and accessories from the 1940s, 1950s, and 1960s. Although the focus is on casual clothes—it bothers Najat that party clothes are frequently very fragile—you can find the odd party gown on her racks. "Wearing vintage is more than just a private pleasure for the wearer; it's to please others as well," says Najat.

Besides clothes, there is a large selection of accessories, from shoes and bags to caps, ties, buttons, fabric, socks, and so on. Unused dresses from the period sell for between €30 and €150. Good-quality suits are between €200 and €450. She sources her clothes from all over France, and over the years she has come across several dead stocks, i.e. unused surplus stocks. Although Najat herself owns a collection of haute couture clothes from the 1930–1970 period, designer clothes are not a priority in her shop.

17, rue Moret, 75011 Paris
Tuesday–Saturday 2 P.M.–7 P.M.
T +33 1 43 57 10 12
M° Ménilmontant

Break

Le Chateaubriand
An excellent restaurant, reopened in 2006 under the direction of Frédéric Penau. The lauded cuisine is by the talented Iñaki Aizpitarte. At lunchtime the food is simple and flavorful, becoming elaborate and fashionable for dinner. Be prepared to book well in advance.
129, avenue Parmentier, 75011 Paris
Every day except Sunday, Monday, and Saturday lunch
T +33 1 43 57 45 95
M° Goncourt or Parmentier

Brigitte Campagne

Brigitte Campagne is unique in the center of Paris for specializing in clothes dating from the beginning of the nineteenth century to the 1940s. She has always been fascinated by the image of women as seen through the history of fashion, and her work is tied to the documentation of women's fashion. After fifteen years outside Paris, in the countryside, she opened this shop in 2002. Sadly, half of the shop and its priceless contents were lost in a fire two and a half years later. But now Brigitte has reopened, with an exclusive selection. Besides clothes, there are all sorts of accessories from the same time period. The specialized nature of her shop attracts a fairly specific clientele, dominated by people from museums, collectors, fashion designers, and costume designers.

It would be a big shame to be put off by the unusual period, however—there are many fabulous creations here that can easily be worn by today's women. Prices start at €10 for certain lace items, and reach €1,000 for some of the dresses. A couple of Brigitte's current favorites are a delightful Paul Poiret top, which was worn by the designer's wife, a waistcoat from Degremont & Bouillon which once belonged to a nobleman, the duc de Noailles, and an exquisite cape from Printemps dated 1907.

17, rue Moret, 75011 Paris
Every day 2 P.M.–7 P.M. or by appointment
T +33 1 43 55 11 98 or +33 6 12 90 56 95 / www.ancienne-mode.com
M° Ménilmontant

Come On Eileen

Pierre Philippe Coiriers has always loved fashion, which he sees as an important part of our cultural history, and is in charge of one of Paris's larger secondhand shops. After about a decade at the Montreuil flea market, the owner opened **Come On Eileen** in 2001. Stand number 898 out at Montreuil is still there, however, handling the surplus from the shop. The focus is on clothes from the period between 1950 and the 1980s, but there are some older clothes, from the 1920s and 1930s, as well. The selection is huge and covers all sorts of designers and styles. And there is plenty for both women and men.

One of the shop's treasures is a jacket by Jean Bouquin once owned by Mick Jagger; other favorites include an early Pucci dress and Paco Rabanne's metal bags. Clothes and accessories come from Paris and the surrounding area. "Why search farther afield when you live in the capital of fashion?" says Pierre Philippe. The selection is replenished three to four times a month. Customers are from all walks of life and all corners of the world. Pierre Philippe has also helped outfit a number of models, actors, and musicians. Prices start at €5 for plastic earrings and reach €400 for furs. A Courrèges dress in excellent condition sells for €120.

16–18, rue des Taillandiers, 75011 Paris
Monday–Thursday 11 A.M.–8:30 P.M.
Friday 11 A.M.–5:30 P.M.
Sunday 11 A.M.–8 P.M.
T +33 1 43 38 12 11
M° Bastille or Ledru Rollin

Les Frères Lumière

In November 2005, Sam Cohen and his brother opened this shop, their second. They are no newcomers, however, with over eleven years in the business. The shop is fairly large. Sam sells clothes and shoes for men and women, with somewhat more choice for men.

There are all types of casual clothes and sportswear, plus quite a lot of military clothes. The selection includes college jackets, army uniforms, motorcycle jackets, leather jackets and coats, football jerseys, classic 1950s baseball jackets, furs, patterned dresses, and masses of sneakers (a large stock of Converse and Jack Purcell originals, for instance). The emphasis is on the 1970s and 1980s, and there are lots of young people among the customers. Prices start at €3 for scarves and peak at €40–50, for furs and leatherwear. Sneakers sell for €39.

Break

Le Réfectoire
A recently opened restaurant
with a short but good menu and
reasonable prices.
80, boulevard Richard Lenoir, 75011 Paris
8:30 A.M.–11 A.M. / noon–2 P.M. /
8 P.M.–10:30 P.M. (closed Sundays in August)
T +33 1 48 06 74 85
M° Richard Lenoir

49, boulevard Richard Lenoir, 75011 Paris
Monday–Saturday 10 P.M.–7:30 P.M.
T +33 1 49 29 03 15
M° Richard Lenoir

Tosca

Tonia is an actress with an overflowing wardrobe. This passion led her to open her tiny shop in 1991. During her years in the theatre, she managed to accumulate an entire theatre wardrobe. When she was touring in Japan, she bought kimonos, and in Romania in the 1960s she picked up folk costumes, and so on. The shop displays clothes from the beginning of the twentieth century and until the present. Tonia herself is fond of the 1940s and of slips. Prices start at €20, which she charges for some skirts and slips. A turn-of-the-century camisole decorated with lace sells for €68. Silk dresses from various decades of the twentieth century are between €60 and €150. An exceptional embroidered silk piano shawl sells for €550. The most expensive item is a jaguar jacket from the 1950s, in mint condition and costing €1,500.

1, rue des Taillandiers, 75011 Paris
Tuesday–Friday noon–7 P.M.
Saturday 2 P.M.–7 P.M. and by appointment
T +33 1 48 06 71 24
M° Bastille or Ledru Rollin

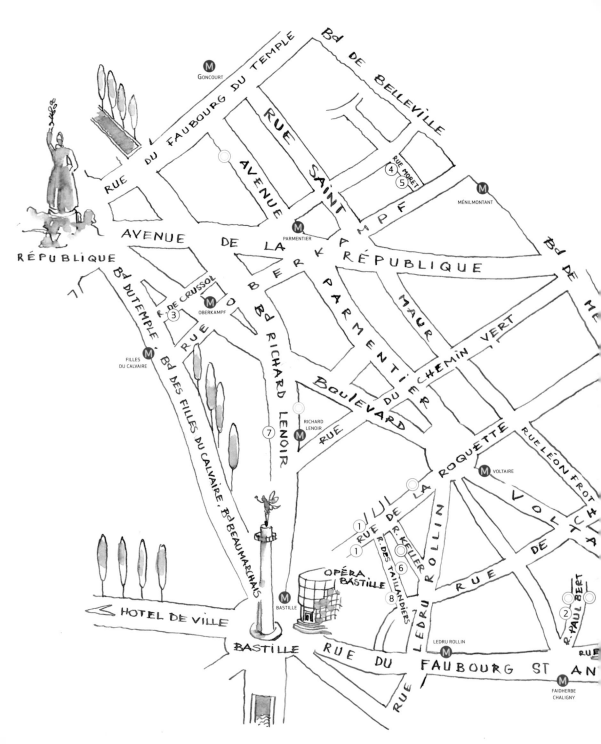

11th arrondissement

Shops

① Adöm
② En Ville
③ Vintage Clothing Paris
④ Casablanca
⑤ Brigitte Campagne
⑥ Come On Eileen
⑦ Les Frères Lumière
⑧ Tosca

Breaks

◎ A la Renaissance
◎ Café Moderne
◎ Unico
◎ Le Bistrot Paul Bert
◎ Le Chateaubriand
◎ Le Réfectoire

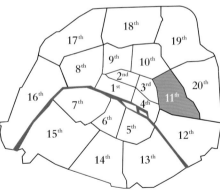

12th & 20th arrondissements

Mme Bijoux

Domenique's main activity at **Mme Bijoux** is renting out clothes and accessories to various theatres and film productions. She has also been making jewelry, hats, and theatre masks for the last thirty years—she made the masks for Sofia Coppola's film *Marie Antoinette*, for example. All the same, she always has a few clothes for sale, dating from the nineteenth century to the 1950s, as well as shoes, hats, jewelry, and other accessories. The period for jewelry is much broader, stretching from the beginning of the twentieth century until the present. Prices start at €15. A nice top from the beginning of the nineteenth century sells for €150, while whole ensembles from the same period cost between €500 and €600.

71, rue de Lyon, 75012 Paris
Monday–Friday noon–7 P.M. (closed the first two weeks of August)
T +33 1 49 28 96 80
M° Bastille

Breaks

**La Maison Rouge/
Fondation Antoine de Galbert**
Not far from Bastille you'll find this red space devoted to contemporary art. It opened in the summer of 2004 and it soon became a must for today's art lovers. There is also a café and a good bookstore.
10, boulevard de la Bastille, 75012 Paris
T +33 1 40 01 08 81 / www.lamaisonrouge.org
M° Bastille or Quai de la Rapée

Swann et Vincent
A very well-liked Italian restaurant with good food in a nice space with a genial atmosphere.
7, rue Saint-Nicolas, 75012 Paris
Every day 11:30 A.M.–2:45 P.M. /
7:30 P.M.–midnight
T +33 1 43 43 49 40
M° Ledru Rollin

R. M Fripes U.S.A

Mick's father owned a wholesale business for importing vintage clothes from America, which Mick eventually took over. Just over ten years ago, he opened his own shop devoted to American fashions from the 1930s until the present. About 70 percent of the selection is menswear, although there are quite a few unisex garments. Mick displays satin smoking jackets from the 1940s and later next to baseball jackets from the glamorous 1980s. Bomber jackets, trench coats, scout's shirts, and camel hair coats share the racks with majorette jackets in bright colors. Embroidered Western shirts from the 1950s and 1970s, and 1940s and 1950s gabardine, flannel, and wool shirts hang beside dress shirts with ruffles. Jeans are piled up next to bundles of military trousers. And everything is in good condition! The shop is on two floors. The lower floor is a combined stockroom and showroom for true enthusiasts. Embroidered Western shirts cost around €60. A dinner jacket sells for around €150, and a matching dress shirt is €40.

108, rue de Lagny, 75020 Paris
Monday–Saturday 11:30 A.M.–7:30 P.M.
Sunday and holidays 1 P.M.–7 P.M.
T +33 1 43 79 38 41
M° Porte de Vincennes

Momo Le Moins Cher

Momo Le Moins Cher ("Momo the cheapest") has been at this address since 1988 and is a classic friperie. The owner has a second shop in the tenth, where the selection of 1970s clothes is somewhat bigger than here. Everything is sorted according to models: Austrian wool jackets, motorcycle jackets, evening dresses, skirts, military clothes, glittery Lurex sweaters, furs, jeans, shoes, crocodile bags, and more. The selection changes with the season. The emphasis is on clothes from the 1970s, 1980s, and 1990s, and there are just as many men's clothes as women's. Prices start at just €1, but quality is not always great. You need to look over your finds closely. Motorcycle jackets are €69, crocodile handbags between €10 and €20, Adidas sneakers between €3 and €20. The highest prices are for furs, costing up to €300–400. Momo also has a wholesale outlet, and sometimes foreign buyers come in and buy up the entire contents of the shop. But don't worry, it soon fills up again.

Breaks

La Boulangerie
A pleasant bistro with well-made French food.
15, rue des Panoyaux, 75020 Paris
Every day except Saturday lunch and Sunday
noon–2 P.M. / 8 P.M.–11 P.M.
T +33 1 43 58 45 45
M° Ménilmontant

Krung Thep
Traditional Thai food. The restaurant is small and rather cramped, so book ahead.
93, rue Julien Lacroix, 75020 Paris
T +33 1 43 66 83 74
M° Belleville

31, rue de Ménilmontant, 75020 Paris
Every day 9:30 A.M.–8 P.M.
T +33 1 43 49 28 16
M° Ménilmontant

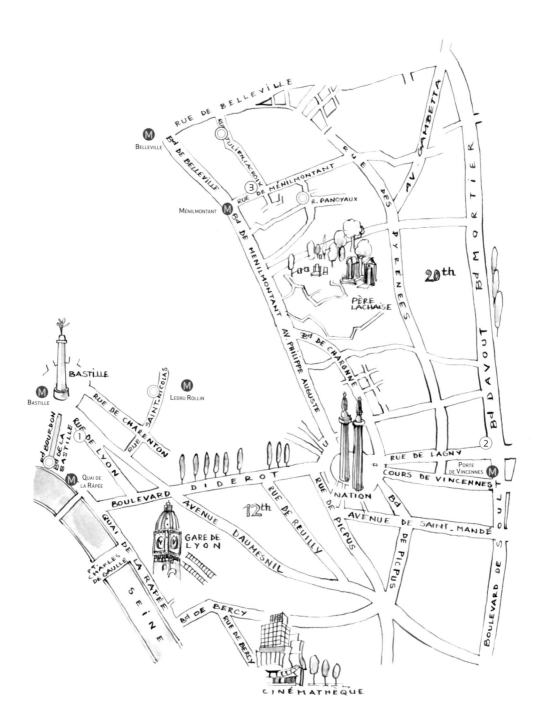

RUE DE BELLEVILLE

M Belleville

Bd DE BELLEVILLE

RUE JULIEN-LACROIX

③ RUE DE MÉNILMONTANT

M Ménilmontant

Bd DE MÉNILMONTANT

R. PANOYAUX

RUE DES PYRENEES

AV. GAMBETTA

Bd DAVOUT

Bd MORTIER

20th

PÈRE LACHAISE

AV. PHILIPPE AUGUSTE

Bd DE CHARONNE

BASTILLE

M Bastille

Bd BOURDON

Bd DE LA BASTILLE

RUE DE CHARENTON

RUE SAINT-NICOLAS

RUE DE LYON

M Ledru Rollin

①

M Quai de la Râpée

QUAI DE LA RAPEE

PT CHARLES DE GAULLE

SEINE

BOULEVARD DIDEROT

AVENUE DAUMESNIL

GARE DE LYON

12th

RUE DE REUILLY

RUE DE PICPUS

NATION

RUE DE LAGNY

COURS DE VINCENNES

②

PORTE DE VINCENNES M

BOULEVARD DE SOULT

AVENUE DE SAINT-MANDÉ

Bd DE PICPUS

Bd DE BERCY

RUE DE BERCY

CINÉMATHÈQUE

12th & 20th

arrondissements

Shops

1. Mme Bijoux
2. R.M Fripes U.S.A
3. Momo Le Moins Cher

Breaks

◎ Swann et Vincent
◎ Krung Thep
◎ La Boulangerie
◎ La Maison Rouge /
   Fondation Antoine de Galbert

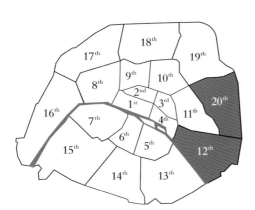

Marché
aux Puces
Saint - Ouen

18th
17th   19th
9th   10th
8th   2nd   20th
1st   3rd
16th   11th
7th   4th
15th   6th   5th   12th
14th   13th

M° Porte de Clignancourt
Bus 85 or 56

Artémise & Cunégonde

Mother and daughter Monique and Clara Lardé have been running this shop for seven years. But more than thirty years have passed since Monique tired of being an engineer and started seeking out lace, linen, and *retro de luxe* full time. That was in the days when it was easy to come across clothes by Poiret, or Sœurs Callot, or Chanel's 1920s creations.

The pair focus on clothes and accessories dating from the 1870s to the 1970s. They are sticklers for quality, so everything is in very good condition. The shop is continuously being replenished from their sizable stocks. Monique has a weakness for the 1920s and 1930s, while her daughter is fond of the 1950s and 1960s.

In addition to clothes, they have a fair amount of bijoux fantaisie by Miriam Haskell, Chanel, Dior, Yves Saint Laurent, Nina Ricci, and Balenciaga, to name a few. The focus is on women, but there are also children's clothes from the turn of the previous century and the early twentieth century. Among their accessories is a large collection of vanity bags and hats from various decades. The vanity bags cost between €120 and €800. The finest and most expensive one is a Napoleon III specimen with exquisite petit point embroidery and a silver buckle. An embroidered Beauvais vanity bag from the 1950s sells for €350. A 1953 haute couture dress by Dior is €5,000. The least expensive are wallets selling for €65.

Allée 1, stand 28
Friday 9 A.M.–noon / Saturday 9 A.M.–6 P.M.
Sunday 10 A.M.–6 P.M. / Monday 10 A.M.–5 P.M.
T +33 1 40 10 02 21 or +33 6 82 17 49 28 (Clara)
www.artemiseetcunegonde.com

Violette / Galerie Farfouillette

Violette can be said to have spent all her life in this shop. Her parents opened **Galerie Farfouillette** in the 1940s. In 1971, she began to sell what were then known as retro clothes, and ever since then, she has spent her time hunting clothes from the past. The period she covers extends over a century, from 1850 to 1950. Her own favorite period is between 1900 and 1930. Among the many treasures, Violette's shelves hold a respectable collection of lace clothes from the turn of the previous century and the early twentieth century. There are clothes and accessories for adults, both men and women, and children—and there is a lot to choose from: lovely children's lace gowns from the early twentieth century, evening dresses, silk slips, tailcoats, frock coats, and workers' clothes. The cheapest items are small pieces of lace and flowers, selling for €1. Ties cost €2–3. Scarves start at €2, but a Hermès is €90. The most expensive item is an enormous, embroidered Spanish silk shawl costing €600.

42–44, rue Paul Bert, 93400 Saint-Ouen
Saturday–Monday 8:30 A.M.–6 P.M.
Tuesday–Friday by appointment
T +33 6 73 10 55 48

Chantal

Chantal has been dealing in antique clothes for more than fifteen years. She has a small but exquisite and exclusive selection of clothes dating from the eighteenth century to the 1950s. Most of the clothes she sells are French.

Not everyone would buy an 1870s dress with a *faux-cul* (bustle) in excellent condition, or a striped silk Revolution coat from Lyon, and her customers are mostly museums, collectors, or inspiration-seeking designers.

Clothes have always interested Chantal, but it was when she was working as a model in New York that she began to take an interest in older items. Besides clothes, she sells accessories, antique textiles, corsets, and lace from the period. She also holds stock, so don't hesitate to ask her if you're looking for something specific.

A Louis XV silk waistcoat with wonderful details, in perfect condition, is priced at €1,200. The same money will buy you a stunning silver-lace wedding dress from the 1920s, with all the accessories included and also as good as new. An easy-wearing Mad Carpentier dress from the 1950s, with a matching bra, sells for €400.

Allée 1, stand 71
Saturday–Sunday 9 A.M.–5 P.M. (open some Mondays)
T +33 1 40 11 09 29 or +33 6 81 31 99 53

Sarah

Like her mother Violette (see **Galerie Farfouillette**, pages 164–165), Sarah grew up in the world of flea markets, surrounded by fabulous creations. This background is clearly reflected in her own exquisite collection of clothes, accessories, and fabrics. After having worked for several years with Violette, she opened her own shop here in 1991. Her focus is on everything to do with women, from the beginning of the nineteenth century until 1950—elegant, extravagant, and chic women, that is. Here you'll find the clothes and accessories these women wore and the fabrics they used to beautify their homes—and also marvelous needlework by women over the past few centuries.

There are 125 large, well-organized boxes and 50 or so smaller boxes for all sorts of accessories and details: pieces of lace in different colors and styles, lengths of embroidered edging, cords and ribbons, encrustations, socks, gloves, corsets, pearl appliqués, patterned fabric, shawls, flowers, and feathers. The shop is a real treasure trove for anyone seeking inspiration, or material to repair an old heirloom. The cheapest items are buttons costing 10 cents each; the most expensive is a *manteau en Irlande* from the previous turn of the century, priced at €1,500. Flowery 1930s evening dresses of silk and crepe sell for €500–600.

Enter via 27, rue Lécuyer or 18, rue Jules Vallés,
Saturday–Monday 10 A.M.–7 P.M.
Tuesday–Friday by appointment
T +33 6 08 01 80 89 / www.chezsarah.fr

Le Monde du Collectionneur

Silvie Bris took over the business here in the autumn of 2003. It is a small shop, specializing in *prêt-à-porter luxe* (ready-to-wear) from designers such as Yves Saint Laurent, Nina Ricci, Hermès, and Givenchy. The clothes are from the 1950s and later, with the majority from the 1970s and 1980s. Silvie also collects crocodile bags and other accessories made of the same type of leather.

Stand 9
Enter via 27, rue Lécuyer or 18, rue Jules Vallès,
Saturday–Monday 10 A.M.–7 P.M.

© HERMÈS

Falbalas

In January 2006, after several years in the business, husband and wife Erwin and Françoise de Fligué opened their first shop. Erwin began collecting vintage clothes as a fourteen-year-old. He bought up everything he could find dating from the end of the eighteenth century to the 1950s. His wife is no less of a collector, even if she began a little later in life. It was these ever-growing collections that came to form the foundation for their shop. In it, you'll find clothes dating from the end of the eighteenth century to the 1960s. The bulk of the clothes are from 1900 until the 1950s, however. There are clothes for both men and women, but women's wear dominates. Most of the selection is bought in France, except when the couple have been on a buying trip to Britain or Italy. There is also a fairly large selection of accessories, plus their own shoe label, l'Astragale—designed and inspired by older models. Designers and costume designers frequently make the pilgrimage here, along with many other lovers of vintage. Among the couple's favorites at the moment is a collection of haute couture dresses from the 1930s, by stars Madeleine Vionnet and Maggy Rouff. Another is an exquisite dress from Worth. Usually these sorts of gems are sold almost as soon as they arrive.

The clothes are always carefully selected, with a certain individuality and an advanced sense of quality. The couple try to keep a reasonable price range, from €10 to €400, though rarities usually cost more.

First floor, stand 284–285
Saturday–Monday 10:30 A.M.–6 P.M.
T +33 6 89 15 83 82 or +33 6 31 23 80 99
www.falbalas.eu

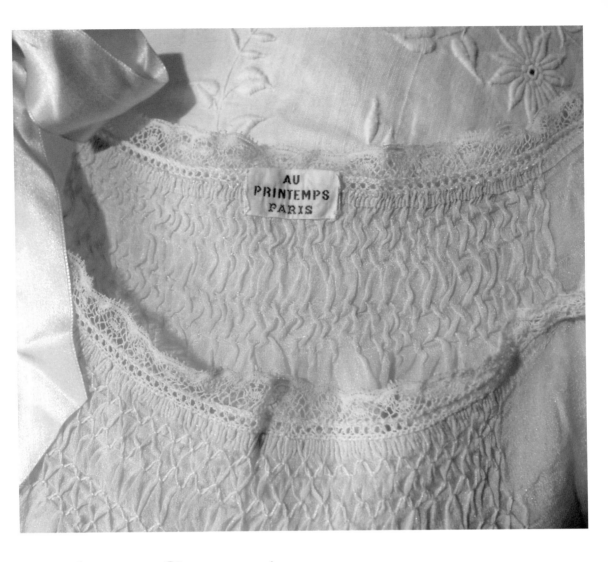

Jacqueline Sainsère Antiquités

Jacqueline's shop is not specialized in clothes, but she has some antique lace garments, older children's clothes, doll clothes, and antique folk costumes from the Middle East and central Europe. Prices for children's clothes are between €50 and €400.

First floor, stand 206
Saturday–Monday 10 A.M.–6:30 P.M.
T +33 1 40 12 42 36

Just Looking

Husband and wife Claude and Jacqueline Guinjard opened their shop here in January 2007. They specialize in fur coats and designer accessories. Jaqueline has been making finds since she was eighteen, until her own closet was ready to burst. The pair focus on the period from 1940 to 1990, but most of the items in the shop are from the 1970s and 1980s. Shoes sell for between €45 and €85; bags for between €125 and €350.

First floor, stand 235
Saturday–Monday 10:30 A.M.–6 P.M.
T +33 6 61 19 46 81

Daniel & Lili

This is a mecca of accessories, an object hunter's paradise, a treasure-house stuffed full of everything you could imagine. Under the same roof, you'll find umbrellas, glasses, shawls, key rings, pens, appliqués, Bakelite necklaces, Galalith necklaces, plastic necklaces, wooden necklaces, paste necklaces, bijoux fantaisie by Chanel, earrings, bracelets, rings, feathers, combs, hats, buckles, toys, ribbons, lace, buttons, pearls, and much more.

For decades, husband and wife Daniel and Lili have sought out and bought up old stocks dating from the 1860s to the 1980s. Most of the objects have been manufactured in France, but there are also things from other countries. The shop has been here for just over twenty years, but the couple have been in the business twice that long. Prices start at 5 cents and reach €400.

At Marché Vernaison (allée 1, stand 6) they have a second shop, **Lili et Daniel**. It is smaller and has a narrower focus than the treasure trove here. The speciality there are pearls and *passementerie* (decorative textile trimmings and edgings).

Ground floor, stand 128
Saturday–Sunday 9:30 A.M.–6 P.M. / Monday 10 A.M.–6 P.M.
T +33 1 40 10 83 46 or +33 1 40 12 01 24
www.lilietdaniel.com

Lucette Pistre

Lucette Pistre has always dealt in antiques. Her mother was haute couture seamstress Irene Haflon, so switching to vintage clothes, as she did in 2002, was not a difficult choice. She specializes in furs, designer clothes, and accessories for women. The period covered extends from the 1950s until the present, but most of the selection are from the 1970s and 1980s. Prices start at €20, for jewelry. A gray 1970s Yves Saint Laurent dress with pearls will cost you €600. Furs cost from €150 all the way up to €4,000, but for the higher price, we are talking about a Christian Dior in good condition.

Allée Sainte-Sophie, stand 65
Friday 9 A.M.–noon / Saturday–Monday 10 A.M.–6 P.M.
T +33 6 23 94 59 59 or +33 1 39 83 20 85

Vakana

Maroulla opened here in October 2004 and has chosen to focus on women's wear and accessories. Most of her items date from 1920 to 1970, but she also has older tops from the end of the nineteenth century. The selection is quite large, and prices are reasonable.

First floor, stand 200-201
Sunday–Monday 10 A.M.–6 P.M.
T +33 6 64 83 87 32

Denyse

Denyse moved her activities here from Rouen fourteen years ago. She spends her weekdays seeking out clothes and accessories all over France. Along with Violette and Sarah, she has one of the bigger vintage shops out here. Denyse deals only in women's clothes and accessories dating from the end of the eighteenth century to the 1960s. She also sells antique textiles and lace. Her selection is varied, and everything is of high quality. Denyse does her buying based on her own taste, but sometimes she will buy something that she feels could be an inspiration for designers. The rows of angora sweaters and leather tops from the 1980s—a style that would not normally appeal to her—and the antique Tibetan costumes are examples of this finely tuned sense of style. The majority of her customers are designers, from near and far. Goodies such as turn-of-the-century dresses, evening gowns from the 1930s, or pearl dresses from the 1920s, in good condition, usually cost around €600. Pretty 1960s cotton dresses can sell for around €160. Silk slips cost around €60, and embroidered cotton granny blouses from early last century around €15.

Allée 2, stand 83
Saturday 10 A.M.–5:30 P.M. / Sunday 10 A.M.–5 P.M.
T +33 1 49 45 14 36

Françoise Schuler

Françoise specializes in antique textiles, but she also has a certain amount of antique and older clothes. There aren't many, but they are all exquisite and unusual items. The time period extends from the eighteenth century until the 1930s. Besides European clothes, she has embroidered garments from China, Japan, and Indochina, plus suits and costumes from North Africa and the Middle East. A French eighteenth-century dress in excellent condition sells for around €3,000, embroidered men's coats and waistcoats from the same era cost between €500 and €1,000, as do pearl dresses from the 1920s.

⌒⌒

Allée 1, stand 33
Saturday–Monday 9:30 A.M.–6 P.M.
T +33 1 40 12 56 65 or +33 6 07 08 64 83
www.antictex.com
dschuler@club-internet.fr

Irma

Irma has had her shop here for twelve years. She does not deal exclusively in clothes, but she has quite a few women's clothes dating from the late nineteenth century until the 1930s. Her husband, André, has a stand at the Montreuil flea market. Together they tour the country during the week, looking for one-of-a-kind clothes and objects. André's selection of clothes is more extensive than his wife's, though Irma also sells lace and linen from the same period.

She charges around €150 for a lace blouse from the turn of the century, while a silk slip from the same era costs about €100. A 1930s dress in good condition sells for between €500 and €600. The cheapest items are white cotton camisoles, at €20.

Allée 9, stand 200
Saturday–Monday 8 A.M.–6 P.M.
T +33 1 40 10 08 57

Break

Chez Louisette (Richard and Armand)
One of the last *guinguettes* (small, unpretentious cabarets / restaurants / dance venues outside the center) in Paris. Has been here since the 1930s. Live music on weekends.
130, avenue Michelet, 93400 Saint-Ouen
(Marché Vernaison, allée 10)
Saturday–Monday
T +33 1 40 12 10 14

Francine

Francine has been here for over twenty years. She has a background as a designer, and began collecting linen and children's clothes for inspirational purposes. Today she has two stands here and a showroom in the fourth arrondissement. Although her main focus is on antique textiles and linen, she also has a lot of clothes and accessories. The clothes date from 1870 to the 1940s. At Francine's you can pick up theatre costumes, the late-eighteenth-century embroidered and pearl-strewn capes known as visites, embroidered silk Manila shawls from Spain, Egyptian 1920s Asyut shawls with their typical silver appliqués, pearl-decorated 1920s dresses, Chinese suits from the 1930s, silk slips, men's waistcoats from 1910 to the 1930s, children's clothes from 1900 to the 1920s, turn-of-the-century dresses, and much more. Francine has extended the time period a tad for hats and accessories—these include the 1950s. Children's clothes cost between €60 and €150. A Manila shawl sells for €500, as do pearl dresses from the 1920s. Men's waistcoats cost between €130 and €200. A richly decorated visite shawl is priced at around €300.

Allée 7, stand 121–123 and stand 140 bis
Saturday 9 A.M.–6 P.M. / Sunday 10 A.M.–6 P.M. / Monday 10 A.M.–5 P.M.
T +33 1 40 10 93 36 or +33 6 07 41 99 01

Antiquités Becker

Valerie Becker has a vibrant collection of jewelry made of Bakelite and other materials, dating from the 1950s and later. She has had this spot only since 2000, but has collected jewelry all her life and studied gemmology when she was younger. Prices range between €10 and €200 for bijoux fantaisie, but for genuine goods such as diamonds and other precious stones, you may have to part with as much as €2,500.

Allée 9, stand 237
Saturday–Monday 9:30 A.M.–6 P.M.
T +33 1 40 10 99 60 or +33 6 12 15 61 82

Martine

Martine has had her tiny but charming and well-filled shop for just over ten years. In it, she sells a little bit of everything, dating from 1920 to the 1970s. She has a lot of accessories, particularly shoes in good condition. You will find a few designer labels at Martine's, but they are not something she goes out of her way to find. Clothes cost from €10 to €200; shoes start at €30. A pair of unused Charles Jourdan from the 1970s sells for €78.

139, rue des Rosiers, 93400 Saint-Ouen
Saturday–Monday noon–7 P.M.
T +33 6 15 15 76 80

R de Paris

Yaneli Delorme is a real fashion aficionado, which is why she opened her small shop here in August 2007. She specializes in women's and children's clothes and accessories from the 1960s, 1970s, and 1980s. Yaneli has built up a colorful collection in which she freely mixes high and low. A collection of less expensive, nondesigner clothes hangs on a rack outside the shop, while designer dresses rub shoulder pads inside the shop. Dresses without labels sell for €35–75, but if it's a Courrèges you are after, you will have to cough up €400.

123, rue des Rosiers, 93400 Saint-Ouen
Friday–Monday 10 A.M.–5:30 P.M.
T +33 6 27 33 16 16

Break

La Chope des Puces
A tiny bistro with *jazz manouche*, or Gypsy jazz, and *moules* (mussels). *Manouche* concerts every Saturday and Sunday between 2 P.M. and 7 P.M.
122, rue des Rosiers, 93400 Saint Ouen
T +33 1 40 11 02 49

D.B.

Delphine's tiny space is crammed full of treasures dating from the eighteenth century to the 1960s. She has been here for just over a decade; before settling here, she mostly travelled around to various fairs. Eighteenth-century silk waistcoats hang from the ceiling, next to white dresses for girls, lace blouses, and embroideries from the turn of the previous century. Behind these are a pearl dress from the 1920s, gleaming black visite capes from the 1870s, and an 1830s dress in mauve-colored Thai silk next to haute couture gowns by Dior and Nina Ricci. A 1930s dress by Madeleine Vionnet hangs next to a creation by Lucien Lelong. The shelves sag under the weight of linen and lace. Haute couture dresses sell for between €500 and €1,500. A 1920s pearl dress costs around €450. The above-mentioned 1830s dress has a price tag of €1,000.

137, rue des Rosiers, 93400 Saint-Ouen
Friday 9 A.M.–11 A.M. / Saturday–Sunday 9 A.M.–6 P.M.
T +33 1 49 48 03 29
delphine@delphinevernaison.net

Chris Fantaisie

For more than twenty years, Chris Brémontier has sought out clothes and accessories dating from the 1890s to the 1980s. Mostly she finds clothes and hats (one of her passions) for women, but she also has men's clothes at the back of the shop. One of the walls is decorated with wonderful evening gowns from the first three decades of the twentieth century. Everything she buys is restored if damaged, the idea being that you should be able to wear all your purchases on the same evening. Chris's shop is the biggest vintage shop on the street. Prices start at €15 and reach €1,000—provided you are not looking at some rarity, in which case they can go even higher.

154 bis, rue des Rosiers, 93400 Saint-Ouen
Saturday–Sunday 10 A.M.–6 P.M. / Monday 11 A.M.–4:30 P.M.
T +33 6 12 96 71 93

Lolotte Vintage

Laure Hervieu has finally found a space. For half a decade, she has led an itinerant existence, travelling around with her wares to faithful customers—mainly vintage shops and designers. She specializes in women's shoes and bags, but also has women's clothes and other accessories. The period covered extends from the 1920s to 1980, but unfortunately the selection thins out at the older end. Laure herself cheerfully mixes different styles and has not pledged herself to any particular period—instead she says there are gems in all of them. She only receives customers by appointment, but she is very flexible about times, so don't hesitate to book with her. Her price range is reasonable. Shoes cost between €35 and €75; bags between €20 and €75. She has about five hundred pairs of shoes in the shop, and about four hundred bags. Twice a year she sells off her stock at half price at a brocante in the third arrondissement.

23, rue Rabelais, 93400 Saint-Ouen (outside the flea market)
Only by appointment
T +33 1 40 11 51 26 or +33 6 11 55 42 95
lolottevintage@yahoo.fr
M° Mairie de Saint-Ouen

There are several fripes along rue Jean-Henri Fabre and rue Jules Vallès, most of them focused on the 1960s, 1970s, and 1980s. Menswear is as well represented as women's wear. Selections are seasonal, and are renewed every weekend. All the owners have been in the business for some time, and they keep more or less the same price levels. These typically start at €2–5 for ties and belts. An Adidas jacket sells for €25–45; corduroy jackets are €25–60. Burberry trench coats vary between €60 and €270. The most expensive items are fur coats, which can cost up to €400. Rue Jules Vallès also has several shops selling military uniforms and their specific accessories.

Monsieur Boulot

A small stand on the left side, toward the autoroute. A fairly typical selection is complemented by fur coats and shoes.

24, rue Jean-Henri Fabre, 93400 Saint-Ouen
Saturday–Monday 10 A.M.–6 P.M.

Petit Michèle

Differs slightly from the other friperies in that there are theatre costumes and party gowns in addition to the usual selection.

41, rue Jules Vallès, 93400 Saint-Ouen
Saturday–Monday 10 A.M.–6 P.M.

Léa Fripes

Two shops along the same street—the first and the last fripe. Consequently, the selection is large and varied, including more leather jackets than many others. In the last shop, at No. 58, they sell their seconds even cheaper!

9 and 58, rue Jean-Henri Fabre,
93400 Saint-Ouen
T +33 6 71 46 22 59

Foxy

In addition to clothes, this largish shop specializes in shoes, boots, and cowboy boots. Prices for shoes are between €35 and €55; boots sell for €58–78.

53, rue Jules Vallès, stand 6–7, 93400 Saint-Ouen
T +33 1 40 10 14 01 / www.foxystand.net

Monica Fripes

Monica's shop used to be on rue Jules Vallès, where she had lots of theatre costumes. She moved to this location three years ago, and she calls this her depot. The selection is a bit different from the other fripes along the street. Monica has some older clothes, accessories, and jewelry—but her theatre clothes have already been sold out. Prices are mostly in the €10–100 range.

58, rue Jean-Henri Fabre, 93400 Saint-Ouen
Saturday–Monday 10:30 A.M.–7 P.M.
T +33 6 80 23 08 07

Roberto Friperie

A fairly large selection of Burberry trench coats, and some designer items. Lots of menswear.

60, rue Jules Vallès, 93400 Saint-Ouen
Saturday–Monday 10 A.M.–6 P.M.
T +33 6 22 67 55 16

Richie Vintage

Two stands next to one another. Richie has lots of clothes and boots from the 1960 to the 1970 mixed with new stuff.

53, rue Jules Vallès, 93400 Saint-Ouen, Marché Malik
Saturday–Monday 10 A.M.–6 P.M.
T +33 6 10 99 04 66

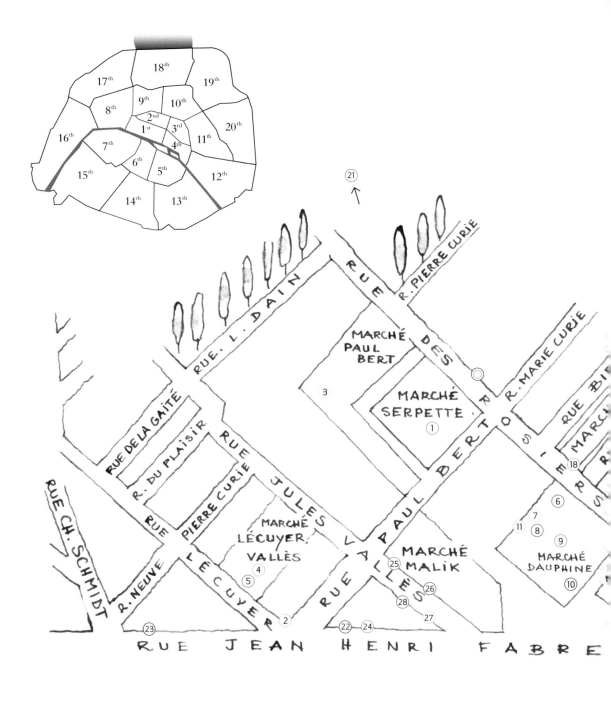

17th
18th
19th
8th
9th
10th
2nd
1st
3rd
20th
16th
7th
11th
4th
6th
5th
12th
15th
14th
13th

21

MARCHÉ PAUL BERT

MARCHÉ SERPETTE
1

3

RUE PIERRE CURIE
R. MARIE CURIE
RUE BIE

MARCH
18

6

7
11
8
9

RUE L. DAIN

RUE DE LA GAITÉ
R. DU PLAISIR
RUE PIERRE CURIE
RUE

MARCHÉ LÉCUYER, VALLÈS
4

MARCHÉ MALIK

25
26
28
27

MARCHÉ DAUPHINE
10

RUE CH. SCHMIDT
R. NEUVE
LÉCUYER
R. PAUL BERTON

JULES VALLÈS

5

2

23
22
24

RUE JEAN HENRI FABRE

MARCHÉ AUX PUCES
SAINT-OUEN

Shops

① Artémise & Cunégonde
② Violette / Galerie Farfouillette
③ Chantal
④ Sarah
⑤ Le Monde du Collectionneur
⑥ Falbalas
⑦ Jacqueline Sainsère Antiquités
⑧ Just Looking
⑨ Daniel & Lili
⑩ Lucette Pistre
⑪ Vakana
⑫ Denyse
⑬ Françoise Schuler
⑭ Irma
⑮ Francine
⑯ Antiquités Becker
⑰ Martine

⑱ R de Paris
⑲ D.B.
⑳ Chris Fantaisie
㉑ Lolotte Vintage
㉒ Monsieur Boulot
㉓ Léa Fripes
㉔ Monica Fripes
㉕ Petit Michèle
㉖ Foxy
㉗ Roberto Friperie
㉘ Richie Vintage

Breaks

◎ Chez Louisette
◎ La Chope des Puces

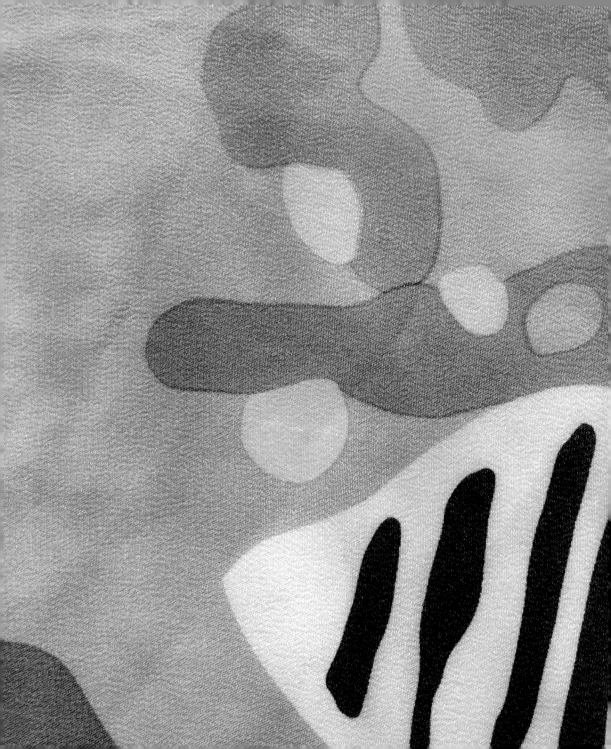

Marché
aux Puces
Montreuil

M° Porte de Montreuil

F. Bonnot
CHAPELIER
92. Bd des Batignolles
PARIS

Anne & Mara

If you are crazy about hats, Anne and Mara will sort you out. Their stand selling hats from the 1880s up to the present has been here since the summer of 1985. If you are looking for a particular hat, you can phone the ladies and they will dig out what you are looking for and bring it to the stand on the weekend.

Handmade silk and lace hats from the end of the nineteenth century sell for €150-200, while the famous Christian Dior's collection of 1947 are €40-50. An Italian boater from the Extra label sells for €60. A silk-lined *melon* (bowler) by F. Bonnot in Paris, from the turn of the last century, costs €80. You can also find lovely hats for as little as €20.

Stand 793
Saturday–Sunday 9 A.M.–7 P.M.
T +33 1 43 79 34 20

Annie Huet

Annie Huet has had her stand here since 1981. It is a large and spacious stand, and each weekend, she displays between two and three thousnd garments for men and women. The time period covered extends from the beginning of the twentieth century until the 1980s, but most of the clothes are from the 1950s, 1960s, and 1970s. Annie has a fondness for strong colors and patterns. She has picked up quite a few dead stocks over the years, so many of the garments are unused. Designer clothes from the likes of Dior, Chanel, Pucci, and Hermès sell instantly, so if it's these labels you are after, you have to get up bright and early on a Saturday morning. Prices start at €3 for clothes you rummage your way through the piles for. 1960s dresses sell for between €30 and €40; coats between €80 and €150.

Stand 834
Saturday–Monday 8 A.M.–6 P.M.
T +33 1 45 44 74 63 or +33 6 89 47 44 70

Société New Puces

Nicole Journo has been here for over thirty years, and this is a stand for finds—at least if you listen to many of Paris's vintage shopkeepers. Here at the market, she sells clothes and theatre costume seconds dating from the 1880s to the 1960s. There is nothing here for men, but just about everything a woman could wish for. Nicole's real treasures are not brought here, however—instead they may be inspected at another location, by appointment. She brings new things to her Montreuil stand every weekend. Usually there are about five hundred garments for sale. Nicole's explanation for the turnover is that "this is not a place to sell things at high prices." On one table is a large pile of clothes where each garment costs between €1 and €5. An exquisite patterned silk kimono from the 1930s sells for €40. Napoleon III black capes cost between €50 and €90. Shoes can be found for €20.

Stand 795
Saturday–Sunday 9 A.M.–6 P.M.
T +33 6 61 45 82 13

Annie Pousset

Annie Pousset ended up here by chance in 1976, when she was selling mostly retro clothes. In the early 1980s, she stumbled upon a stock of shoes from the 1940s, and since then shoes and boots dating from the 1940s until the 1980s have become her speciality. She stills sells clothes as well, mostly from the same period and mostly for women—except for leatherwear, which is for men. Prices range from €10 to €150; dresses cost between €10 and €50. Every weekend, Annie displays around two hundred pairs of boots and cowboy boots, priced between €50 and €100. Shoes are even more numerous—usually Annie displays between two and three hundred pairs at a time, priced between €40 and €45.

Stand 797
Saturday–Sunday 9 A.M.–6 P.M.
T +33 1 45 42 63 09 or +33 6 13 51 90 89

Nadine

Nadine has always loved women's clothes made from light fabrics that move in the wind and follow the body's movements. Her preference is reflected in the feminine, light, and delicate selection she unpacks here every weekend, dating from the late nineteenth century to the 1980s. Nadine opened her stand here in 1980. Her collection is vast, and doesn't change that much with the seasons. Among the things you'll find here are lace blouses from the previous turn of the century, pink and cream-colored silk blouses from the 1930s and 1940s, dresses and slips from the turn of the century and later. The garments in the pile on the table sell for between €5 and €15. Scarves cost between €2 and €30. Dresses start at €20, but a very elegant 1930s silk dress will set you back €700.

Stand 832
Saturday–Sunday 10 A.M.–5 P.M.
some Mondays 10 A.M.–5 P.M.
T +33 6 08 53 53 01

Irma

André "de Montreuil" (as he is known) is married to Irma "de Clignancourt" (see page 183). For thirty years, in all weathers, he has unpacked and repacked his wares every weekend. At André's you'll find clothes from the nineteenth century until the 1960s, plus fabrics. There are both men's and women's clothes, and the selection is renewed every weekend. André buys his clothes together with his wife, all over France and Belgium. He also has quite a few designer clothes, including Dior and Pierre Cardin, but demand for these is very great, so you need to get there early. Prices start at €10 for blouses; slips are priced from €15. A fabulous fur coat sells for €400.

Stand 794
Saturday–Monday 8 A.M.–6 P.M. (closed from
August 15 until the second week of September)
T +33 6 60 44 08 77

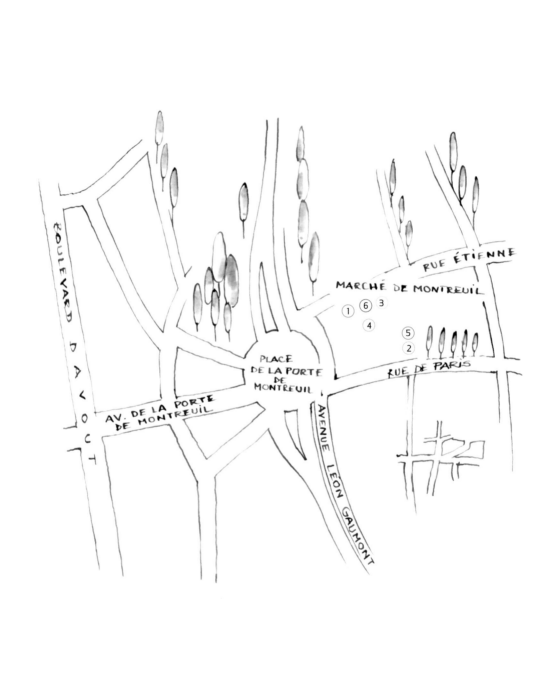

BOULEVARD DAVOUT

RUE ÉTIENNE

MARCHÉ DE MONTREUIL

① ⑥ 3

4

⑤

2

PLACE
DE LA PORTE
DE
MONTREUIL

AV. DE LA PORTE
DE MONTREUIL

RUE DE PARIS

AVENUE LÉON GAUMONT

MARCHÉ AUX PUCES
MONTREUIL

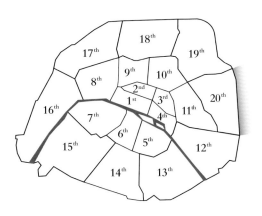

Shops

1. Anne & Mara
2. Annie Huet
3. Société New Puces
4. Annie Pousset
5. Nadine
6. Irma

More Vintage

For more information about flea markets

The flea markets open during the weekends. Official flea market hours are from 8 AM. If you're a serious shopper, try to get there early, as it becomes very crowded after lunch! It is also good to bring cash, as stallholders seldom accept credit cards and the nearest available ATM always has a line.

Apart from these regular flea markets, so-called brocantes or travelling flea markets and *vide-greniers*—literally, attic emptiers; French garage sale, in other words—are put up in and around Paris every weekend. For information on when and where to find them, check out these websites:

www.iledefrance.org

A site for the Île de France, the area around Paris. Under art/culture, you will find where and when the brocantes and vide-greniers are held in and around the city.

www.pointsdechine.com

A French site with a timetable for brocantes and vide-greniers all over France.

www.parispuces.com

A site regarding the flea market in Saint-Ouen.

www.vide-greniers.org

A French site where you can find information about where and when there is a brocante or a vide-grenier in France.

www.fiftiessound.com

Organizes vide-greniers several times per year. The address is always:
11, cour Debille, 75011 Paris
M° Voltaire

www.aladinmag.com

A magazine with information about brocantes in France.

www.mairie-lille.fr

Use this site to find out when and where the Braderie de Lilles, a popular flea market, is held every year in September in the city of Lille.

Useful Web sites for online vintage shopping

www.vintagemartini.com

In addition to their online shop, they also have a shop in Carrollton, Texas.

www.mintandvintage.com

A Swedish site with English text. Besides their online shop, they have shops in Stockholm and Helsingborg in Sweden.

www.poshgirlvintage.com

Posh Girl Vintage is family owned and operated in southern California.

www.lilyofthevalley.se

A Swedish site with English text. Run from Jönköping, Sweden.

www.1860-1960.com

Mother and daughter Beth and Julie Guernsey run this US-based online vintage shop.

www.mamastonevintage.com

An online shop for women. "Dresses from 1960s Mod, Twiggy, Space-Age, Victorian, Dolly, Lolita, Baby doll, 1970s Disco, Hippie, Peasant, Boho, Bohemian & 1980s."

www.adorevintage.com

An online shop with vintage clothes from the 1950s to 1980s.

www.tastyvintage.com

An online shop run by Harriet, who is based in Lincoln in the UK. Vintage clothes from the 1930s to the 1970s.

www.bysolange.com

A French vintage online clothing shop. Specializes in vintage luxury couture, haute couture, and secondhand clothes from the 1950s to the1980s.

www.vintagetrends.com

This online shop "was created to be the leading web-based distributor of vintage, military, recycled and designer clothing and accessories." It is based in southern California.

www.vintagevixen.com

Shop and order online at this vintage clothing shop with a huge selection and variety of clothing from the Victorian era to the 1970s.

www.unique-vintage.com

Offers bargain to designer vintage clothing from collectible and antique apparel to designer and haute couture.

www.shopnastygal.com

Very inspired by the 1980s and 1990s.

www.ballyhoovintage.com
A great place to get vintage clothing from the 1930s to 1970s for men and women.

www.rustyzipper.com
Vintage disco, flares, bellbottoms, Hawaiian shirts, dresses, bowling shirts, denim, and sewing patterns, 1940s through 1970s.

www.kittygirlvintage.com
Women's vintage clothing from the 1920s to 1970s including accessories, shoes, and jewelry.

www.vintage70sclothing.com
Specializes in offering unusual vintage clothing, shoes, and accessories from the 1970s, 1960s, 1950s, and 1940s for women and men.

www.vintageous.com
Vintage clothing, costume jewelry, and fashion accessories from the 1940s to 1950s and beyond, including formal wear and casual wear.

www.monstervintage.com
Vintage clothing for men and women, with over one hundred categories.

www.thewaywewore.net
Vintage clothing and retro costumes; 1940s swing dresses, 1950s cocktail dresses, 1960s clothing, 1970s disco clothing, and poodle skirts.

www.sydneysvintageclothing.com
Vintage dresses, hats, purses, shoes, and suits from the 1930s to the 1980s.

www.fireflyvintage.com
A unique collection of rare and collectible vintage clothing.

www.antiquedress.com
Features the beauty and elegance of original clothing from the 1800s through today, including Victorian ensembles, Edwardian whites, and 1920s flapper dresses.

Blogs

http://vintage-folie.over-blog.com

http://poshgirlvintage.blogspot.com

The author and the publisher assume no responsibility for the consequences arising from use of these sites.

Contacts

1st

Neila Vintage & Design (p. 12)
28, rue du Mont Thabor
T +33 1 42 96 88 70
jaziri_neila@yahoo.fr
M° Tuileries

Didier Ludot (p. 14)
Jardins du Palais Royal,
20 and 24, Galerie Montpensier
T +33 1 42 96 06 56
www.didierludot.com
M° Palais Royal Musée du Louvre

La Petite Robe Noire (p. 16)
Jardins du Palais Royal
125, Galerie Valois
T +33 1 40 15 01 04
M° Palais Royal Musée du Louvre

Iglaïne (p. 18)
12, rue de la Grande Truanderie
T +33 1 42 36 19 91
iglaine@wanadoo.fr
M° Les Halles or Etienne Marcel

Gabrielle Geppert (p. 20)
Jardins du Palais Royal,
31 and 34, Galerie Montpensier
T +33 1 42 61 53 52
or +33 6 22 92 53 25
www.gabriellegeppert.com
M° Palais Royal Musée du Louvre

Création & Diffusion Rag (p. 22)
81, rue Saint-Honoré
T +33 1 40 28 48 44
M° Les Halles

Son & Image (p. 24)
85–87, rue Saint-Denis
T +33 1 40 41 90 61
M° Les Halles

Fr/Jp Design & Vintage (p. 25)
8, rue La Vrillière
T +33 1 42 96 11 48
www.frjp-boutique.com
fr.jp@wanadoo.fr
M° Bourse

2nd

Oldies (p. 26)
25, rue de Cléry
T +33 1 42 33 21 28
www.myspace.com/oldiesvintagclothes
M° Sentier

Vintage 39–41 & 51–53 (p. 28)
39–41, passage Choiseul (women)
51–53, passage Choiseul (men),
T +33 1 42 96 64 79
vintageshop3941@yahoo.fr
M° Quatre Septembre or Pyramides

Kiliwatch (p. 30)
64, rue Tiquetonne
T +33 1 42 21 17 37
www.kiliwatch.fr
M° Etienne Marcel

 3rd

Yukiko (p. 36)
97, rue Vieille du Temple
T +33 1 42 71 13 41
www.yukiko-paris.com
or www.vintage-paris.com
M° Saint-Sébastien Froissart

Marie Louise de Monterey (p. 38)
1, rue Charles-François Dupuis,
T +33 1 48 04 83 88 or +33 6 73 87 69 46
www.marielouisedemonterey.com
M° Temple

La Jolie Garde-Robe (p. 40)
15, rue Commines
T +33 1 42 72 13 90 or +33 6 80 91 33 55
M° Filles du Calvaire

Chez Dentelles (p. 42)
16, rue Rambuteau
T +33 1 42 74 02 51
M° Rambuteau

La Belle Epoque (p. 44)
10, rue de Poitou
T +33 6 80 77 71 32
M° Saint-Sébastien Froissart

La Licorne (p. 46)
38, rue de Sévigné
T +33 1 48 87 84 43
M° Saint-Paul

Studio W (p. 48)
6, rue du Pont aux Choux
T +33 1 44 78 05 02 or +33 6 10 66 14 66
studio.w@free.fr
M° Saint-Sébastien Froissart

Planète 70 (p. 50)
147, rue Saint-Martin
T +33 1 48 04 33 96
M° Rambuteau

Olga (p. 51)
45, rue de Turenne
T +33 1 42 72 44 92
olgashop@hotmail.com
M° Saint-Sébastien Froissart

Pretty Box (p. 52)
46, rue de Saintonge
T +33 1 48 04 81 71
M° Filles du Calvaire

Son & Image (p. 24)
71, rue Quincampoix
T +33 1 42 79 16 89
M° Rambuteau

 4th

Mamz'Elle Swing (p. 58)
35 bis, rue du Roi de Sicile
T +33 1 48 87 04 06
www.mamzelleswing.fr
M° Saint-Paul

Free P Star (p. 60)
8, rue Sainte Croix de la Bretonnerie
T +33 1 42 76 03 72
M° Hôtel de Ville

Sélima Optique (p. 62)
46, rue Vieille du Temple
T +33 1 48 04 38 55
M° Saint-Paul or Hôtel de Ville

Vintage Désir (p. 63)
32, rue des Rosiers
T +33 1 40 27 04 98
M° Saint-Paul

A l'Elégance d'Autrefois (p. 64)
5, rue du Pas de la Mule
T +33 1 48 87 78 84
M° Chemin Vert

Fuchsia Dentelle (p. 66)
Corner of rue de l'Ave Maria
and rue Saint-Paul
T +33 1 48 04 75 61
M° Sully Morland, Saint-Paul,
or Pont Marie

Francine (p.68)
5, rue de l'Ave Maria
T +33 6 07 41 99 01
M° Sully Morland , Saint-Paul,
or Pont Marie

Vertiges (p. 70)
85, rue Saint-Martin
T +33 1 48 87 34 64
M° Rambuteau

Le Photon des Vosges (p. 71)
9, rue du Pas de la Mule
T +33 1 42 77 45 22
M° Chemin Vert

Fripes Star (p. 72)
61, rue de la Verrerie
T +33 1 42 78 00 76
M° Hôtel de Ville

Rag (p. 74)
83, rue Saint-Martin
T +33 1 48 87 34 64
M° Rambuteau

6th

Aurélie Antiquaire (p. 80)
12, rue de l'Echaudé
T +33 1 46 33 59 41
M° Mabillon or
Saint-Germain des Prés

Ragtime (p. 82)
23, rue de l'Echaudé
T +33 1 56 24 00 36
or +33 6 16 10 35 35
francoise.auguet@noos.fr
M° Mabillon or
Saint-Germain des Prés

Les Trois Marches de Catherine B.
(p. 84)
1, rue Guisarde
T +33 1 43 54 74 18
or +33 6 74 98 17 25
www.catherine-b.com
M° Mabillon

7th

La Renaissance (p. 86)
14, rue de Beaune
T +33 1 42 60 95 49
www.renaissance75007.com
M° Rue du Bac

8th

Scarlett (p. 96)
10, rue Clément Marot
T +33 1 56 89 03 00
M° Franklin D. Roosevelt

Les Antiquaires de la Mode (p. 98)
3, rue Chambiges
T +33 1 47 20 56 19
M° Franklin D. Roosevelt

9th

Wochdom (p. 108)
72, rue Condorcet
T +33 1 53 21 09 72
wochdom@hotmail.com
M° Anvers or Pigalle

Chezel (p. 110)
59, rue Condorcet
T +33 1 53 16 47 31
M° Anvers or Pigalle

Ménage à 3 (p. 112)
9, rue Clauzel
T +33 1 48 78 44 80 or +33 6 77 15 71 68
www.menage-a-trois.fr
M° Saint-Georges or Pigalle

Anouchka (p. 114)
6, avenue du Coq
T +33 1 48 74 37 00
M° Saint-Lazare

Chic Office (p. 116)
19, rue de la Grange Batelière
T +33 1 48 01 04 36
M° Richelieu Drouot
or Grands Boulevards

Showroom
31, rue Saint-Lazare
T +33 1 40 26 83 59
M° Notre Dame de Lorette

Mamie (p. 118)
73, rue de Rochechouart
T +33 1 42 82 09 98
www.mamie-vintage.com
M° Anvers

Mamie Blue (p. 120)
69, rue de Rochechouart
T +33 1 42 81 10 42
www.mamie-vintage.com
M° Anvers

Guerrisol (p. 122)
17, boulevard Rochechouart
T +33 1 45 26 13 12
M° Barbès Rochechouart

10th

Guerrisol (p. 122)
45, boulevard de la Chapelle
M° Barbès Rochechouart

Quidam de Revel (p. 124)
55, rue des Petites Ecuries
T +33 1 42 71 37 07 or +33 6 10 04 97 80
www.quidam-de-revel.com
M° Poissonnière, Château d'Eau,
or Bonne Nouvelle

Zôa (p. 126)
55, rue de Lancry
T +33 1 44 52 01 67
www.zoa.fr
M° Jacques Bonsergent

11th

Adöm (p. 132)
35 and 56, rue de la Roquette
T +33 1 43 57 54 92 or +33 1 48 07 15 94
M° Bastille

En Ville (p. 134)
13, rue Paul Bert
T +33 1 43 71 07 30
M° Faidherbe Chaligny

Vintage Clothing Paris (p. 136)
10, rue de Crussol
T +33 1 48 07 16 40 or +33 6 03 00 64 78
www.vintageclothingparis.com
M° Oberkampf or Filles du Calvaire

Casablanca (p. 138)
17, rue Moret
T +33 1 43 57 10 12
M° Ménilmontant

Brigitte Campagne (p. 140)
17, rue Moret
T +33 1 43 55 11 98 or +33 6 12 90 56 95
www.ancienne-mode.com
M° Ménilmontant

Come On Eileen (p. 142)
16–18, rue des Taillandiers
T +33 1 43 38 12 11
M° Bastille or Ledru Rollin

Les Frères Lumière (p. 144)
49, boulevard Richard Lenoir
T +33 1 49 29 03 15
M° Richard Lenoir

Tosca (p. 146)
1, rue des Taillandiers
T +33 1 48 06 71 24
M° Bastille or Ledru Rollin

12th

Mme Bijoux (p. 152)
71, rue de Lyon
T +33 1 49 28 96 80
M° Bastille

14th

Magic Retour (p. 88)
36, rue de la Sablière
M° Pernety

15th

Doursoux (p. 90)
3, passage Alexandre
T +33 1 43 27 00 97
www.doursoux.com
M° Pasteur

16th

Nuits de Satin (p. 100)
5, rue Jean Bologne
T +33 1 45 27 27 45
www.nuitsdesatin.com
M° La Muette or Passy

17th

Stéphane (p. 102)
65, place du Docteur Félix Lobligeois
T +33 1 42 26 00 14
M° Rome or La Fourche

Guerrisol (p. 122)
19, avenue de Clichy
T +33 1 40 08 03 00
M° Place de Clichy

18th

Guerrisol (p. 122)
21, boulevard Barbès
M° Château Rouge

20th

R.M Fripes U.S.A (p. 154)
108, rue de Lagny
T +33 1 43 79 38 41
M° Porte de Vincennes

Momo Le Moins Cher (p. 156)
31, rue de Ménilmontant
T +33 1 43 49 28 16
M° Ménilmontant

Puces de Saint-Ouen

Artémise & Cunégonde (p. 162)
Marché Serpette, allée 1, stand 28
T +33 1 40 10 02 21
or +33 6 82 17 49 28 (Clara)
www.artemiseetcunegonde.com

Violette / Galerie Farfouillette (p. 164)
42–44, rue Paul Bert
T +33 6 73 10 55 48

Chantal (p. 166)
Marché Paul Bert, allée 1, stand 71
T +33 1 40 11 09 29
or +33 6 81 31 99 53

Sarah (p. 168)
Marché Lécuyer Vallès,
Enter via 27, rue Lécuyer
or 18, rue Jules Vallès
T +33 6 08 01 80 89
www.chezsarah.fr

Le Monde du Collectionneur (p. 170)
Marché Lécuyer Vallès, stand 9
Enter via 27, rue Lécuyer
or 18, rue Jules Vallès

Falbalas (p. 172)
Marché Dauphine,
first floor, stand 284–285
T +33 6 89 15 83 82
or +33 6 31 23 80 99
www.falbalas.eu

Jacqueline Sainsère Antiquités
(p. 174)
Marché Dauphine,
first floor, stand 206
T +33 1 40 12 42 36

Just Looking (p. 175)
Marché Dauphine,
first floor, stand 235
T +33 6 61 19 46 81

Daniel & Lili (p. 176)
Marché Dauphine,
ground floor, stand 128
T +33 1 40 10 83 46 or +33 1 40 12 01 24
www.lilietdaniel.com

Lucette Pistre (p. 178)
Marché Dauphine,
allée Sainte-Sophie, stand 65
T +33 6 23 94 59 59 or +33 1 39 83 20 85

Vakana (p. 179)
Marché Dauphine,
first floor, stand 200-201
T +33 6 64 83 87 32

Denyse (p. 180)
Marché Vernaison, allée 2, stand 83
T +33 1 49 45 14 36

Françoise Schuler (p. 182)
Marché Vernaison, allée 1, stand 33
T +33 1 40 12 56 65 or +33 6 07 08 64 83
www.antictex.com
dschuler@club-internet.fr

Irma (p. 183)
Marché Vernaison, allée 9, stand 200
T +33 1 40 10 08 57

Francine (p. 184)
Marché Vernaison,
allée 7, stand 121–123, stand 140 bis
T +33 1 40 10 93 36 or +33 6 07 41 99 01

Antiquités Becker (p. 186)
Marché Vernaison, allée 9, stand 237
T +33 1 40 10 99 60
or +33 6 12 15 61 82

Martine (p. 188)
139, rue des Rosiers
T +33 6 15 15 76 80

R de Paris (p. 190)
123, rue des Rosiers
T +33 6 27 33 16 16

D. B. (p. 191)
137, rue des Rosiers
T +33 1 49 48 03 29
delphine@delphinevernaison.net

Chris Fantaisie (p. 192)
154 bis, rue des Rosiers
T +33 6 12 96 71 93

Lolotte Vintage (p. 194)
23, rue Rabelais
(outside the flea market)
T +33 1 40 11 51 26 or +33 6 11 55 42 95
lolottevintage@yahoo.fr

Monsieur Boulot (p. 197)
24, rue Jean-Henri Fabre

Léa Fripes (p. 197)
9 and 58, rue Jean-Henri Fabre
T +33 6 71 46 22 59

Monica Fripes (p. 197)
58, rue Jean-Henri Fabre
T +33 6 80 23 08 07

Petit Michèle (p. 197)
41, rue Jules Vallès

Foxy (p. 197)
53, rue Jules Vallès, stand 6–7
T +33 1 40 10 14 01
www.foxystand.net

Roberto Friperie (p. 197)
60, rue Jules Vallès
T +33 6 22 67 55 16

Richie Vintage (p. 197)
Marché Malik, 53, rue Jules Vallès
T + 33 6 10 99 04 66

Puces de Montreuil

Anne & Mara (p. 202)
Stand 793
T +33 1 43 79 34 20

Annie Huet (p. 204)
Stand 834
T +33 1 45 44 74 63 or +33 6 89 47 44 70

Société New Puces (p. 205)
Stand 795
T +33 6 61 45 82 13

Annie Pousset (p. 206)
Stand 797
T +33 1 45 42 63 09 or +33 6 13 51 90 89

Nadine (p. 208)
Stand 832
T +33 6 08 53 53 01

Irma (p. 210)
Stand 794
T +33 6 60 44 08 77

THIS BOOK WAS CREATED BY

2, cité Dupetit Thouars
75003 Paris

EDITORIAL CONCEPTION / DIRECTION
Catherine Bonifassi / Jessica Clayton

DESIGN
Sabrina Regoui

PHOTOGRAPHS BY
Jessica Clayton, © Cassi Edition

MAPS DESIGNED BY
Vincent Structure, © Cassi Edition

TRANSLATION
Tomas Tranæus

SEPARATIONS
Cassi Edition / LC Photogravure

Although every effort has been made to ensure that the information in
this book is as up-to-date and as accurate as possible at press time, some
details are liable to change.

First published in the United States of America in 2009 by
Universe Publishing
A Division of Rizzoli International Publications, Inc.
300 Park Avenue South
New York, NY 10010
www.rizzoliusa.com

ISBN: 978-0-7893-1863-3

Library of Congress Control Number: 2008932316

2009 2010 2011 2012 / 10 9 8 7 6 5 4 3 2 1

Printed in China